FACE TO FACE

Conversations with my Father

Joseph Schickel

TO JOSEPH PLUT WITH GRATITUDE

Joseph Schickel

John tells us of a city so high up above

Where we meet in the spirit of love

When we meet over yonder, in that heavenly place.

There, we'll see each other, face to face.

From the old Biblical folk song *Lights of the City*,
rediscovered, arranged, and recorded by Ed
Gutfreund.

FACE TO FACE

CONVERSATIONS WITH MY FATHER

Joseph Schickel

William Schickel Gallery
200 W. Loveland Ave.
Loveland, Ohio 45140

To Susie and our boys,

with love and gratitude.

TABLE OF CONTENTS

Acknowledgements

My thanks go first to Paula Huston, whose assistance with this project through *Glen On Line*, a program of the journal *Image*, was absolutely essential and invaluable. Donna Barnes, Elizabeth Murphy, Paula Oguah, Joy France, Candi Schickel, Sarto Schickel, Mary Wlodarski, Pia Alm-Basu, William Skudlarek, OSB, and Joseph Plut reviewed draft manuscripts and offered helpful comments and many corrections.

Ron Hansen and Gretchen Kresl Hassler, widow of the author Jon Hassler, gave words of support, and their generous permission to use excerpts from *Exiles* and *North of Hope*.

My sons, Will, Tom, and Charlie were outstanding caretakers for their Grandfather. They also corrected many errors of fact in this book, and agreed to tolerate my version of events in a few instances.

My wife Susie's amazing generosity of spirit, first with Dad, then helping me with this book, is the miracle of my born days. She is a voracious reader, not easily impressed with written words. She endured the struts and frets of several miss-starts, then held the bar a little higher, and urged me to go for it.

"But I need encouragement," I whined, before

skulking back to the basement, and getting off my ass. Susie considers this book her fourth child, another big-headed boy. She is a very lucky girl—and today I will buy her flowers.

Introduction

Dad's care after Mom died was a team effort, and luckily we had the dream team. We quickly found out what Mom had doubtless known—that Dad was pretty high maintenance in his older years. She made it look effortless, fooling some of us, or at least me, into thinking Dad's care would be easier than it was. It made us appreciate her, and what she had been doing, all the more.

Shortly after Dad came to live with us, a visiting neighbor asked him if he had any advice for old age.

"Have children," smugged the father of eleven.

"A self-serving statement, if I ever heard one," I muttered under my breath. Susie looked at me, rolled her eyes, smiled sweetly and knowingly, and went to get Dad's glass of red wine.

My wife, Susie, and sons, Will, Tom, and Charlie were outstanding caregivers. I will always be grateful for their generosity and good cheer in bringing Dad into our home.

The Loveland crew put on a full court press. My sisters Elizabeth (Lebe) Robinson and Joy France, and brothers Benedict and Martin played major roles in Dad's daily care. Numerous visits from grand-daughters (Dad's not mine!) Amanda Heisler and Eva

France brightened his days. Brothers-in-law John Robinson and Steve France provided much front line and behind the scenes support. My brother John stayed at our house with Dad several times when we took family trips and vacations, and this was a tremendous help. And a whole raft of more distant siblings, cousins, grandchildren, great grandchildren, nieces, nephews, friends, and fans showered Dad with visits, phone calls, pictures, notes, and gifts—which made his world go round.

Good neighbor awards go to Mary Ellen Camele, Donna Barnes, Paula Oguah, and Pat Hill. The good folks at Cindy's Friendly Tavern and Lohrum's Gym kept an eye on Dad when he made the rounds. Caregivers Peg O'Callahan (who is an amazing fiddler) and Fran Amico, and Physical Therapist Laurie Ray did far more than their jobs required. The steady friendship and support of Father Anthony Dattilo and the Stone family were invaluable.

As a family we stretched and grew by having Dad with us. We got a lot more than we gave, as I hope this book will show. Thanks, Dad.

FACE TO FACE

Conversations with my Father

1. Kitty Hawk, 2007

It was a glorious summer day, and our 1999 Pontiac Montana minivan ambled down Highway 158, looking a little lost. Susie and I rode up front; the three boys were in back. It was our first visit to the Outer Banks and it was a bit overwhelming. The sky was blue and big waves pounded the beach. It was beautiful.

"Oh my God, did you see that bird?" yelled Charlie, our twelve-year-old. I had seen it. Above the surf a pelican hovered in the sea breeze, then folded its wings and plummeted head first a hundred feet into the water, then emerged again with the tail of a good sized fish flapping fast, furious, and futile from the edge of its deep bill.

"That was amazing," I said. "Please say oh my *gosh*."

"Look at those waves," said Tom, our fourteen-year-old. Our three boys loved big waves, and these were definitely bigger than the ones we had seen on the Jersey shore. They had their Boogie Boards ready.

"The restaurant is called Five Guys," said Will, our sixteen-year-old. "It's in Kill Devil Hills and it has really good burgers and fries."   I glanced in the rearview mirror. Will's eyes were fixed on the screen of his cell phone. He grunted and texted furiously. There were white ear buds in both ears.   His thick head, butt, torso, and limbs occupied fully half of the space in the back of the van, and were arranged for maximum comfort and minimum dignity. One of his football buddies, no doubt a beefy lineman, was texting him fine dining information for the Outer Banks.

"Five Guys? What kind of name is that?" asked Tom.

"It sounds like the story of my life," said Susie, but we ignored her, having more pressing matters on our minds. Really good burgers and fries!   Susie looked bleak.

We stopped in the middle turn lane of Highway 158, the main north/south highway of the Outer Banks, attempting to turn left into the cluster of windswept buildings where Five Guys was located. It was our first day on the Outer Banks and I did not yet fully appreciate the gravitas of making a left turn on 158. Our van rocked precariously in the wind of a passing eighteen wheeler which almost blew us into oncoming traffic.

"Why don't these idiots slow down?" I growled. "It's vacation for God's sake."

"Say for *gosh* sake, Dad," said Tom.

SUSIE AND I SAT IN BEACH CHAIRS and watched the boys play in the surf. It was endlessly enjoyable to watch them when they were getting along. Will and Charlie tossed the football. Tom waded out into the surf, then retreated laughing when big waves smacked him around.

"I think I made a scene at Costco," Susie said.

I HAD BEEN AT THE FIREHOUSE, three months earlier, when I learned that Mom was in an ambulance, in critical condition, on her way to the emergency room. Driving to the hospital I had called

Susie.

"I didn't want to tell you there, but I didn't know what else to do," I said. "I needed you to get home to be with the boys."

"I understand," she said. "The ladies at Costco were very sweet and helpful. They got me settled down and straightened out."

A big wave smacked Tom and his arms flapped furiously as he struggled to keep his balance.

"My very first thought was that Dad would be moving in with us," she said. Her second thought had been to bring big trays of Costco sandwiches to the hospital for the gathering family.

"Everybody was sure that Dad would die first," I said.

In the phone calls to extended family and friends shortly after Mom's death, my siblings and their spouses experienced the same thing. The party being called, noting the serious tone of the call, jumped mentally ahead and expected to hear that Dad had died. A few seconds later, when they heard it was Mom, they were totally shocked.

Mom was a youthful seventy-six and Dad's caretaker when she died suddenly and unexpectedly. Dad, then eighty-seven, weighed a number of options, and accepted our offer to move into our home.

To our thinking it made sense. We had a large ground floor room Dad could use, with its own outside entrance, room for a wheelchair ramp, and a good place to add his own separate bathroom. The room was big enough to set up a work area where he could paint, since he was still very active as an artist. I could do telephone and computer work in my basement bunker, directly beneath Dad's room, so I could hear and keep an eye on Dad on my non-firehouse days. Our house was about a mile from the house Dad and Mom had lived in, so he could keep his circle of friends and acquaintances. With the separate outside entrance he would have some autonomy. He could come and go on his own to the extent he was able. He could have visitors without coming into the rest of the house. As a Cincinnati Firefighter I had extended periods of time off—so I could be home and care for him a good bit of the time. Our three boys were growing up. They could help with things like transportation and other care. Susie and I really valued the idea of the boys getting to know their grandfather better.

It had been something of a family joke (a joke to me anyway) that it was always *Susie and the guys*. She grew up with two brothers. In her work as music director at a Catholic church she was often the only woman among clergy. She had a husband, three sons, and now a father-in-lawg to live with and care for. We were about to become the house of Susie and Five Guys. Sometimes I had to remind her how lucky she was!

Dad and I had been close for many years. He was an artist, and I had been his agent, promoter, and assistant for a long time. I started helping him out in the shop when I was in grade school. I liked working with him, partly because it gave us time to talk, and I really liked talking with him. We talked about family stuff and making ends meet. We talked about the art commissions and design projects we were working on. We talked about Reds baseball, Moeller football, and the Bengal Bouts boxing tournament at Notre Dame.

We talked about art, religion, literature, and politics. Dad knew his mind about most things. He knew his mind and his stuff when it came to art and religion. He had some great teachers at Notre Dame —Frank O'Malley, Yves Simon, James Withey, Thomas Stritch—and through them learned about Jacques Maritain's philosophy of art.

Dad once gave a talk at Saint Olaf College in Minnesota and shared the stage with Ben Shahn during a question and answer session. A philosophy professor in the audience suggested that something Shahn had said "contradicted the principles of aesthetics." Shahn walked to the edge of the stage before unloading on the chin scratcher: "Aesthetics is to the artist as ornithology is to the birds!" he bellowed.

I started reading the books Dad talked about and then we would talk further. I got a good, if somewhat spotty education in some rarified subjects. There aren't many firemen who know 'bout dis stuff.

We were headed into uncharted water as a family. Was this really a good idea? For us? For Dad? What were we getting ourselves into? For how long? It was one thing for me—flesh and blood—quite another for Susie as daughter-in-law. Dad and Mom were married for sixty years—and always had their own home. The idea of living without Mom and in someone else's home would be a huge adjustment for him. Would he be happy? Would he be cheerful?

THE SEA BREEZE WAS GETTING CHILLY and we prepared to go. The boys gathered their things and we walked back to the van.

"He was your best friend," said Susie as we walked.

"You mean my best friend after you," I replied.

Susie rolled her eyes. Whatever.

"I just hope he's happy living with us," I said.

"We really don't know what we are taking on," said Susie.

"Or for how long. It could be a year. It could be ten years." I said.

"It could be more than ten years," said Susie. "And I want you to know that I'm fine with this. I *want* to do it. I'm a little scared, and feel guilty that we didn't do it for my Dad, but I really want to do it. It will be good for us as a family."

We shook off the sand and got back in the van.

"Now let's get some dinner," Susie said. "I'll pick the place, and it won't be a burger joint."

Joseph Schickel

2. Morning

I was just off the firehouse and heading home. It was a beautiful morning, crisp and cool, and the sun was making a majestic entrance on Riverside Avenue in Loveland, Ohio. Some of its good rays melted frost on the east side of the sycamore trees on the Loveland Bike Trail. Others visited and stirred up minnows and catfish at the bottom of the Little Miami River. A few hit the dashboard of my '99 Ford Taurus as I pulled into our driveway.

And one shit-stirring independent-minded little sunbeam named *Ray*, pulled off an amazing logistical feat. He had casually left the surface of the sun eight minutes earlier. Slipped out the back. He quietly penetrated the earth's atmosphere on the morning of 7 September 2007. At 0751 hours he threaded his way through several tangles of tree branches on the west bank of the Little Miami River. He passed about twenty feet above a yellow school bus which was stopped in front of our house. A sixth grade boy wearing a grey hooded St. Columban sweat shirt was getting on the bus.

Ray slithered through the porch screen, refracted and changed his angle slightly as he passed through the thick glass of the front window. And finally he skipped off the polyurethane on a wood board in the hall and landed full force in the left eye of an 87-year-old man sitting in a chair, blinding him as he attempted to set his coffee cup down on the little table by his chair.

"Oh dammit; I made a mess!" Dad cried, as the coffee cup clattered to the floor.

Susie came running from the kitchen. "Don't worry, Dad, it's no big deal," she said, as she wiped up the coffee, and replaced the unbroken cup on the table. Invisible *Ray* stuck around just long enough to enjoy his accomplishment. He smiled to himself, and then slipped out the back.

"Susie, could you open the bathroom door, that sun is blinding me!" Dad said.

"Sure, Dad, sorry about that," said Susie. She propped the bathroom door open to block the sun coming down the hall so it wouldn't get in his eyes. This was the third time she had propped the door open. The hallway was a main thoroughfare of activity as the boys got ready to go to school.

Susie had been up since six o'clock—getting the boys off to school, getting Dad's day started, getting ready for my arrival home, and getting her own teaching day organized in her head. Will was in high school, and left at 6:50. Charlie's bus came at 7:50, about the same time I got home from the firehouse. Susie and Tom left for Leaves of Learning, a home school enrichment program where Susie taught and Tom was a student, at about 9:00.

My firefighting schedule was 24 hours on duty followed by 48 hours off. I started work at 7:00 a.m. and got off at 7:00 a.m. the following day. I would leave the house at 6:00 a.m. before work, and get home a little before 8:00 the following morning. This meant that Susie did most of the morning routine with Dad two days out of three in my three-day work cycle. This included waking him, setting out his clothes, steadying him as he made his way into the dining room (he used a cane in those early days), getting his coffee and breakfast, sitting next to him and discussing the day, doing the scripture readings, administering his morning medications, eating breakfast with him, slipping out to empty his portable urinal and clean his room, steady him when he went back to his room. That was the minimum. It's enough to keep a smokin' lady hoppin' when she is also: (1) getting three teenage boys off to school, (2) getting ready for work herself, and (3) making herself radiant to welcome home The Joe.

Dad was a morning person and liked to be up and in the flow while the boys were getting off to school. If you let him sleep too late he got upset. The morning was a time of pretty intense activity, and it could be dicey taking care of Dad and getting the boys off to school.

I WAVED TO CHARLIE'S BUS DRIVER, picked up the *Cincinnati Enquirer* from the front yard, and headed inside.

"Good morning!" I said, closing the bathroom door yet again as I came down the hallway.

"Good morning, sweetheart, how was your night?" Susie inquired from the kitchen.

"Only one run after midnight," I said.

"Susie, could you open the bathroom door, that sun is blinding me," Dad said.

Susie sent a playful stares of accusation at me as I hurried to prop the bathroom door open again. I was the one who had closed the bathroom door, and I was standing right next to it while Susie was ten feet away in the kitchen. But Dad asked *her* to go open it. She had been playing steppenfetchit for grandpa for twenty-four hours while I was at the firehouse—and was happy to start schleppin' the steppin' now that I was on the scene.

I sat down next to Dad and pulled the *Enquirer* out of the plastic bag. Dad was hard of hearing. To have a conversation with him you had to sit very close.

"What's the main headline?" he asked as I perused the front page.

"President Bush is negotiating with North Korea over nuclear arms," I said.

"Read that again," Dad said. I started to read it again. He put his hand to his right ear.

"Dammit, I left my hearing aid in my room," he said.

"I'll get it," I said quickly, cutting him off before he could ask *Susie* to go get his hearing aid. I fetched the hearing aid from his room and handed it carefully to him. He put it in, then held his head still, which was the signal for me to speak.

"Is it working?" I asked. "Testing, one, two, three …"

"It's working," Dad said. "I can hear you fine."

"Should we do today's readings?"

"I would like that."

And so it happened. In the Year of Our Lord Two Thousand and Seven, on Tuesday of the Twenty-Second Week in Ordinary Time (Cycle A), in the town of Loveland, Ohio, on the banks of the Little Miami River, at the CHURCH OF WHAT'S HAP'NIN' NOW!, the Catholic doctrine of the Resurrection of the Body was briefly scrutinized.

The book was opened and the court was adjourned, and Miss Susie, regal in her black robes as First Deaconatrix—raised both arms to quiet the congregation. She got her Deaconatrix training watching Flip Wilson and playing the character Lucy in the play *You're a Good Man Charlie Brown*. She read from First Corinthians:

But if Christ is preached as raised from the dead, how can some among you say there is no resurrection of the dead? If there is no resurrection of the dead, then neither has Christ been raised. And if Christ has not been raised, then empty (too) is our preaching; empty, too, your faith. Then we are also false witnesses to God, because we testified against God that he raised Christ, whom he did not raise if in fact the dead are not raised. For if the dead are not raised, neither has Christ been raised, and if Christ has not been raised, your faith is vain; you are still in your sins.

1 Corinthians 15:13-17

"What are we actually talking about here?" I asked.

"Bodies flying out of graves!" said First Deaconatrix Susie.

"It's a wild faith we believe in," said Dad.

Sleepy-eyed, teen-aged Tom shook his head incredulously as he passed through the room on the way to the basement laundry to find clothes. What are my parents talking about? Why can't we be normal?

"It's a basic teaching of the Church," Susie said. "It's in the Apostles Creed. It says, … *we believe in the communion of saints, the forgiveness of sins, the resurrection of the body, and life everlasting.*"

"Amen!" I said. "Let's have breakfast."

I steadied Dad as he moved to the table. Susie, Dad, and I said grace. Teenage Tom sat and looked grim.

Now that the daylight fills the sky
We lift our hearts to God on high
That he in all we do and say
Will keep us free from harm today

Bless us O Lord and these thy gifts
Which we are about to receive from thy bounty
Through Christ Our Lord, amen

We had cereal, coffee, and juice. Tom and Susie excused themselves, and got ready to leave. Dad and I sat and talked.

"When you have time, I have a list of things I'd like to go over with you," he said. I could see he had the list in his hand, magic marker writing on graph paper.

"Why don't we touch on it briefly now," I said. I wasn't ready for a full-scale meeting. I was just off the firehouse and wanted a little time to regroup. We went through the list together.

ITEM #1 was *What a Woman!*—the book he was writing about Mom with my assistance. He was very eager to keep that moving forward. I said I would do some writing on it in the next few days.

ITEM #2 was the Second Edition of the book *Sacred Passion: the Art of William Schickel* by Gregory

Wolfe. There were numerous editing, photography, and layout matters that I was working on and he was anxious for me to keep it moving. "Is there anything we can do to hurry this along?" he asked.

ITEM #3 was our upcoming trip to Notre Dame for his Lifetime Achievement Award from the American Maritain Association. He wanted to make sure everything was in place for that. He was really hoping that Susie would come.

ITEM #4 was some prescriptions he needed picked up.

ITEM #5 was his desire to get down to the William Schickel Gallery to see the paintings that his grandson, Emil Robinson, had dropped off for an upcoming exhibit. He was a big fan of Emil and his developing artistic career.

ITEM #6 was painting supplies. He was almost out of canvases and several paints. We needed to place an order at Suder's Art Store or make a run down there.

DAD WAS KEEPING ACTIVE, and so was I. I steadied him as he rose from the table, and with his cane tapped his way back to his room.

"Honey, we're leaving, have a good day," Susie said as she and Thomas headed out.

FACE TO FACE

Dad and I talked for a few minutes in his room, and agreed to do a walk and read at 10:00 a.m. He started painting, then took a call from my brother Bill in Iowa, and I left. I got more coffee and headed for my basement bunker to figure out my day.

It was 9:00 a.m. and I had a million things to do.

Pace yourself, Joe.   Pace yourself.

Joseph Schickel

3. Grailville

Dad wanted to visit Mom's grave. We drove east on O'Bannonville Road. Just out of town we came to the 400 acre farm called Grailville. It was operated by a group of lay women called the Grail, which was dedicated to restoring the Christian spirit to all aspects of life. There were rolling pastures with grazing cattle. Fields of corn and soy beans. Gravel roads, tractor paths, and barbed wire fences. A perfectly rounded hill with a wooden cross atop that we called Calvary. Two ponds and lots of trails. A cluster of beautiful old houses, barns, and out-buildings with nearby mature trees. The buildings had literary and philosophical names: Joy, Tidings, Pneuma, Hodie, Caravansery, Oratory.

Mary Alice Frei Schickel, my mother, was born on July 17, 1929, the youngest child of Emil and Alice Frei of St. Louis, Missouri. The Frei family was in the stained glass business. Dad met her when he worked there as an apprentice. Young Mary Frei attended school for a time at Grailville. Dad would hitchhike down to visit her, and they were married there on September 13, 1947. They bought a small farm and Dad began his professional career as an artist and designer. Soon there were children. Mom and Dad lived in Loveland their entire married life of sixty years, and had eleven children.

"When I came to Grailville there were lots of beautiful young women here," Dad said, tugging on the bill of his crusty cap and looking self-satisfied.

"And one in particular," I said.

Dad laughed.

"How do you explain Grailville to people?" I asked Dad.

"You can't," he replied.

This was true. Those of us who experienced Grailville as part of our childhood, who loved and respected it, who laughed at it knowing we were actually laughing at ourselves, who had it in our bones whether we liked it or not, had all been through the conundrum of trying to explain it to the uninitiated. It was difficult!

"It's like jazz, or the blues, or a good joke. If you have to explain it, it's just not worth it," Dad said.

"Kinda like your art," I said.

Dad laughed again. "Maybe so, but that's your problem," he said.

Yes, it *was* a conundrum and it was my job to explain it.

"Art people don't trust you because you're religious," I said.

"And religious people don't trust me because I'm a contemporary artist," Dad said.

"It kinda limits your market, don't you think?"

"Could you turn that heater up, Joe?"

CINCINNATI WAS NEVER BIG ON MODERN ART or architecture. Dad's 1977 downtown wall mural *Seventy Foot Love Letter to the Queen* (Cincinnati is the Queen City), with its anodized aluminum panels and drip paint was one of only a few frankly modern public art commissions in Cincinnati in its era. Most cities of comparable size have more. Ironically it was done by an artist whom art critics are sometimes eager to dismiss because of his Catholic orthodoxy.

Dad's paradoxes confounded many. Modern artist and orthodox Catholic. Drip painting and the Pegboard (more about this in Chapter 4). Germanic discipline and childlike frivolity. Eastern by birth, midwestern by choice. City boy who bought a farm, and learned to milk a cow at age 30, then milked a cow twice a day every day for twenty-five years.

WE WERE HOPING THE GROUND WAS DRY enough to drive to the cemetery. It was a ten minute walk over the hill behind the Oratory. But walking was out of the question for Dad at this point.

"I hope it's dry enough to drive down there," I said to Dad.

"We really don't want to get stuck," Dad said. The hard-wired risk taker did not relish the prospect of getting cold.

"I'm going to leave you in the car for a few minutes while I walk partway down to check the ground," I told him.

"Could you turn that heater up a little bit?" he said.

I parked the car at the top of the hill, cranked up the heater, and walked down the tractor path to check the ground. It was like walking back into my childhood. I checked a couple of low spots. A little wet, but I thought we could make it. I had my cell phone if we really got in trouble. I walked back up the hill, got in the car, and turned the heater down.

"Let's give it a go," I said, and we headed down the hill.

The Ford Taurus shumped along the tractor path. At wet spots I straddled one of the tractor tire's mud ruts to keep my tires in the higher, dryer grass. It felt mushy a few times but we did fine, at least on the way down.

We drove along the edge of a soybean field and came to an arch made of telephone poles that formed an entrance to a large clearing of prairie grass surrounded by trees.

"I remember bailing hay down here," Dad said. "We put it in the barn that is now the Oratory." In the early sixties Dad designed the renovation of this barn into a chapel called the Oratory, which won lots of awards. The monks at Gethsemani heard about it, came to look at it, then hired Dad for their project. It's a stunning work of art, no bias here of course. But if you're ever in southwest Ohio, and have an interest in organic architecture, come see the real deal.

"ANNA AND I USED TO RIDE HORSES DOWN HERE," I said. Anna is my oldest sister.

One side of the clearing was dominated by the large Robert Wilson sculpture called *The Poles*, which had fallen into disrepair. At the opposite end was the cemetery.

We stopped the car by Mom's grave. I popped the trunk, pulled out Dad's wheelchair, unfolded it, and brought it over to him. He was waiting with car door open and legs swung out. Ready to go! Time's a wastin'! I steadied him as he got in the wheelchair. I pulled the wheelchair backwards through the thick grass and onto the gravel by Mom's grave.

The grave marker was a good-sized granite rock. Several people had left flowers, crosses, and hand made-mementos. You could hear the wind in the trees. It was very peaceful.

"It was a beautiful funeral," Dad said. "So many people. Everybody loved Mary."

After a few minutes I told Dad I would leave him alone for a while and then come back. I walked past *The Poles* and tried to find the old road that went down to Shangri La.

Shangri La. Aptly named. Hard to find. Mysterious. Tucked away at the edge of Grailville on a bluff overlooking the O'Bannon Creek. There were lots of stories about it during the sixties when *The Poles* were being constructed. My older brothers joked about the "hippies" who hung out down there and worked on the project. I was too young to go, but old enough to be intrigued.

I found the old road but it was overgrown with head-high weeds. I remember riding up that hill atop a loaded hay wagon in the mud. Veronica Forbes drove the new Massey Ferguson with its shiny red paint, pulling the wagon up the hill through the mud. Deborah Shack drove the old Massey Ferguson and pushed from behind. Several Hill and Schickel kids rode gleefully on top of the hay, cheering and trying to keep bales from falling off. We thought we were "helping" and it's amazing nobody got killed!

I walked back toward the cemetery. Dad was in his prayer zone, head bowed, shaking slightly, lips moving, and hands slightly upraised. I approached slowly.

We said an *Our Father* and a *Hail Mary* together, and then he was ready to go. I wheeled him back to the car and we got in.

"Thank you Joe, I'm very glad we did that," Dad said. I leaned over to help him with the seat belt so the alarm wouldn't go off.

"I enjoyed it," I told him.

We headed back across the fields and up the hill, and I told him I'd better focus on driving if we didn't want to get stuck. He was all for not getting stuck. I gathered speed to get momentum for the muddy spots. The car swiveled and the tires spun in mud, but in a few minutes we were safely back on the gravel road near the Oratory.

"Dad, do you remember when Thomas and I found your caskets in the barn?" I asked him.

"Remind me," he said.

SO I TOLD HIM THE STORY. My son Thomas, age eight at the time, and I had been rooting around in the barn at Mom and Dad's house. It was kind of dark and creepy up in the barn, with junk and lots of cobwebs. Tom has a flare for the dramatic. Maybe he has visited the Loveland Castle too often or seen too many Harry Potter movies. We climbed the ladder that led to the loft. At the top Tom froze, pointed, and said in a slow stage whisper,

"What is that?"

I looked where he was pointing, and at the far end of the loft were two rectangular boxes that could only be coffins or caskets.

"Looks like Mom and Dad had coffins made for themselves," I said to Tom.

"What!?" said Tom wide-eyed and standing stalk still.

I walked over and examined the caskets. They were simple and well made of oak, and looked to be the work of our neighbor Phillip Ping, whose woodworking operation was in the barn that used to be Dad's workshop—a mile down O'Bannonville Road.

Tom was determined to be aghast, and psychologically scarred if possible.

"You take me up here to see my Grandparents' coffins!!!!!!" he said in a tone suggesting child abuse on my part.

Later that day I told Mom about the incident with Tom. She laughed at Tom's reaction and confirmed that Phil Ping had made the coffins for them. Phil used the wood from the big oak tree in their yard which was cut down a few years ago.

A little later as we were leaving, Mom walked outside and talked with Tom.

"I hear you saw our coffins up in the barn," she said to Tom matter-of-factly.

Then she explained to Tom that she and Dad wanted nice coffins made because they were getting older and wanted to be ready, so they hired Phil Ping to make them. She asked Tom how he liked them. He cleared his throat and tried to look matter of fact.

"They look pretty nice," Tom croaked.

Dad laughed and laughed.

"Mary was great that way," Dad said. "She knew just how to handle situations like that."

"LET'S DRIVE DOWN BY THE OLD FARM," I said. We headed down O'Bannonville Road. We went over the O'Bannon bridge, crossed the railroad tracks, pulled into a gravel driveway on the left, and stopped. The old farm was up on the hill in front of us—the house, barn, and tool shed.

"It's a great spot," said Dad. "Could you turn that heater up?" I did.

"Dad, tell me about Dr. Gerson," I said.

"Well, I don't know where to start," he said, "except that you and I wouldn't be here without him." Dad had terminal lymphoma in his early thirties, a few years after he and Mom moved onto the farm. They had three young children at the time. The prognosis was grim. He was given only a few months to live. "We drove up to New York and he took me on as a patient. I started recovering pretty quickly once I started the Gerson Therapy."

"Was it a miracle?" I asked.

"I think the miracle was that Mary found Dr. Gerson."

"Say a little more."

"Well here we were in the middle of nowhere.

No indoor plumbing, no furnace, minimal electricity and telephone. But somehow Mary managed to find one of the few people on the face of the earth who knew how to cure me. It's a miracle."

WE DROVE TO LAROSA'S PIZZA and had lunch together, then came home and Dad said he was ready for his nap. I stuck my head in to check on him as he was dozing off. He must have heard, or more likely sensed, my presence.

"Hey Joe," he said. "Can you check and make sure my coffin is still up there in the top of the barn?"

"Sure, Dad," I said.

"I really miss Mary," he said. "I'm looking forward to seeing her again."

"I guess that wood box is the rocket-ship for your reunion, eh?"

Dad laughed.

"I'll make sure it's still there. Have a good nap."

"Thanks Joe."

4. Pickleville, 1966

It was a warm October evening in 1966 on our farm in Pickleville, the little hamlet of half a dozen houses near the O'Bannon bridge and B&O Railroad crossing east of Loveland. I had a flashlight in one hand and a glass of iced coffee in the other as I walked out to the barn. It was hard for me not to run —I really liked to run—but Mom had implored me not to spill the coffee, so I walked fast. My blue jeans were ripped at the knee. I had a red ball cap on my head, a scapular medal around my neck, a sheath knife on my belt, and a harmonica in my pocket.

"HI, JOE, COME ON UP," Dad called down when he heard me open the Shop door. I crossed the long room, and went up the stairs, and set the coffee down on Dad's table—a sheet of plywood on saw horses.

"Thank you, Joe," said Dad cheerfully. He put a slide into the top carousel on the Kodak projector. "Can I get you to listen to part of my presentation?"

"Sure," I said. "Which project is this for?"

"Kane County Prison," he replied. "It's a new project."

"So you're doing a prison and a monastery at the same time?" I said.

"You sound like the warden," Dad said. "We had a great discussion about that during the interview."

"There are some similarities," I offered.

"Yes, and one big difference," he said. "A monastery is voluntary."

He went through his presentation. He had a short introduction, then showed designs for prison cells and common rooms with drawings on easels and projected slides.

"How did I do?" he asked me.

"I think it's great," I said. I thought it was cool that he was working for a prison.

"Joe, could you get me the latest invoice for Kane

County?" Dad asked. I ran downstairs and opened the file drawer marked "receivables," pulled out the latest invoice, and brought it up to him.

"I think we can send another one," he said, after looking it over. "Can you work on that tomorrow after school."

"Sure," I said.

"Thanks, Joe," Dad said. "Quick game of ping pong?" I ran downstairs and got the paddles out, and we played a quick game.

I LEFT THE SHOP and walked around the barn. I opened the gate, entered the barnyard, and pumped water into the galvanized tub on the concrete slab over the well. Daisy (our milk cow), Patches (my calf), and Snickerdoodle (our beef cow) drank thirstily as I pumped, then followed me into the stall when I opened the barn door. I cut bailing twine with my sheath knife and put half a bale of hay in the trough. While they ate hay, I removed fresh cow pies with a pitchfork, then spread some fresh straw. I shined the flashlight around the barn, enjoying the bar of light in the hay dust.

Our dogs, Ira and Spot, appeared as I walked toward the house. I sat on the post and rail fence overlooking the front pasture, B&O railroad crossing, and O'Bannon bridge. Way down the tracks I could hear a train approaching, big diesels straining on an uphill grade. The dogs lay at my feet. I played Old Black Joe on the harmonica—and went inside.

Joseph Schickel

5. Walk Paint Read

For I greet him the days I meet him, and bless when I
understand.
Gerard Manley Hopkins

I hear artists say they paint what they see.   It's probably a
funny thing to say, but I paint what I think.
William Schickel

"Good morning, Dad," I said as I entered his room. It was midmorning, 10:00 a.m. to be precise, and time for his walk.

"I can't talk right now," he said. He was sitting at his worktable, painting away. A cool-looking blue, black, and red abstract painting was taking shape under the sharp focus of the goose neck light over his table. He stippled black paint onto canvas with a little roll of paper towel. Artist sponges sat unused on the shelf behind him. His black ball cap had spots of red paint, and his arthritic hands were splotched with black and blue. He was engrossed, focused and happy. I watched him paint for a few moments.

"That's a great looking painting, Dad," I said. "I'll come back in a little while."

"Hey Joe, can you do something for me?" he said as I started to leave. "See if you can find another bottle of cadmium red paint over there."

I crossed the room, and searched through the bottles of paint on his shelf. His current painting was a combination of cobalt blue, carbon black, and cadmium red. Dad had a hard time reading the labels at this point, and often needed help finding the color he wanted. I found a bottle of cadmium red, and poured a couple ounces into the dish next to his painting.

"How's that?" I asked.

"Perfect."

"Should we walk in a little while?" I asked. Dad and I took a walk around the block every day (on my non-firehouse days) at 10:00, weather permitting. It was a good routine for him. It structured his day, got him some exercise, gave us a chance to talk, and often gave him good social interaction with neighbors.

"How about in twenty minutes?" he replied. Although phrased as a question it didn't have the feel of a question. We would walk in twenty minutes.

"I'll be back," I said.

When I returned in twenty minutes he was sitting in his rocker ready to roll.

"How cold is it out there?" he asked.

"About seventy," I replied, fetching his jacket from the closet. Dad's room was kept at eighty-three degrees, and seventy would feel cold to him. I helped him put the jacket on, then put his wheelchair outside on the driveway at the bottom of the steps outside his room.

"Is the wheelchair ready?" Dad asked.

"It is," I replied.

I helped him stand up. Then, using grab bars and railings he made his way out the door, down the steps,

43

and into the waiting wheelchair while I watched. His upper body was strong, and he could make his way around if he had good grab bars. His legs were weak.

We called it a walk though he rode in the wheelchair more than half the way.

"I'm excited about that painting," Dad said as I pushed him down the driveway and onto the sidewalk.

"I'm glad you are using plenty of red," I said. Dad was well aware of my ongoing request to have plenty of red in his paintings.

"You do like red, don't you," he said. We turned the corner from Riverside Avenue onto Main Street and stopped for the first of his three actual walks.

"Ready for your warm-up?" I asked. His first walk was short, just to get his legs going.

"Ready," he said.

I turned the wheelchair around, facing backward, then steadied it as he grasped the arm-rails and stood up. He turned himself around and stood facing the wheelchair, steadying himself by holding the arm-rails. Then, using the wheelchair as a walker, he pushed it backward and we walked along the sidewalk together for about twenty feet. I kept my right hand looped loosely through his belt in back so I could catch him if he lost his footing (which did not happen often) and assist him in getting back into the chair when he was done walking (which he needed much of the time).

"Could you pull my cap back?" he asked as we started to walk. It was slipping forward and the bill was starting to cover his eyes. I adjusted his cap as he walked.

"Thank you," he said, slightly out of breath. Walking took all his focus and energy.

"That's it," he said after walking twenty feet. I steadied him with the belt as he turned himself back around and sat down landing heavily in the wheelchair.

"Whew, I'm a bit weak today," he said.

"That wasn't too bad," I commented. "You'll do better on the second leg." Dad's always-changing leg strength was a mystery. Some days it seemed easy. Other days it was hard.

I turned the wheelchair back around, and we headed down the sidewalk again.

"Is Susie working today?" Dad inquired.

"Yes, she's teaching," I replied. He was thinking about lunch. It was going to be just me and Dad for lunch. He much preferred lunch when Susie was there too. Maybe we would go to LaRosa's just to get out a bit more.

"Is there anything we can do to keep Notre Dame Press moving forward?" he asked. The University of Notre Dame Press was releasing the second edition of the book *Sacred Passion: the Art of William Schickel* by Gregory Wolfe. Dad was eager to hurry it along.

"They are waiting on better photos of Gethsemani and Bellarmine," I replied. Dad's designs for the renovations of the Abbey of Gethsemani in Kentucky and Bellarmine Chapel at Xavier University in Cincinnati were featured in the book.

"Is that our responsibility?" Dad asked.

"Yes," I replied.

Silence. The underlying message was, "How are you going to accomplish this?"

"I am hoping to get down to Gethsemani next month," I said. "We did Bellarmine last week."

Bellarmine Chapel at Xavier University was nearby. Though Dad apparently did not remember it, he had come with me for a photo shoot there last week—and the photos had turned out well. The Abbey of Gethsemani was three hours away, and an overnight trip. I needed a minimum of half a day to shoot Gethsemani because light conditions were so changeable there. A full day would be better. The difficulty was Dad's care when I was gone. Susie was already stretched.

As we turned the corner onto Wall Street our neighbor Paula came out and gave Dad a big hug. She patted him on the shoulder, talked loudly and got right in his face as she fussed, coddled, cajoled and called him "Mr. Schickel." He loved it.

"She's a wonderful person," Dad said when she went back in the house. I could tell it really picked up his day.

"Are you ready for your long run?" I asked Dad.

"Ready as I'll ever be," he replied as I turned his wheelchair around. The Wall Street leg was where we measured Dad's distance and progress.

"Here goes," Dad said as he again pushed the wheelchair turned walker backwards along the sidewalk.

"I'm feeling stronger," Dad said, chugging along. And indeed he looked stronger, lifting his feet a little higher and making good progress.

"Push my hat back, Joe," he said, and I adjusted the black ball cap back so the bill would not block his vision.

"You're doing really good, Dad," I said when we reached fifty feet.

"Hey there, Sunny," Dad said, nodding dismissively to a big sunflower next to the sidewalk that he always thought was watching him.

Dad set a new record that day and felt very hopeful about it.

"If I could just get my legs stronger I'd be in pretty good shape," he said. We did his *cool down* walk on the last leg of the block and then returned back inside.

"That was a great walk, Joe, thank you so much," Dad said, back in his room, seated in the rocking chair.

"Should we read some *Exiles*?" I asked Dad.

"Do you have time for that?"

"Let's do about fifteen minutes."

WE SAT IN THE LIVING ROOM and resumed reading *Exiles,* the fascinating new novel by Ron Hansen. It tells the story of the poet Gerard Manley Hopkins (1844-1889) and his epic poem *The Wreck of the Deutschland.* Dad had studied Hopkins with Professor Frank O'Malley at Notre Dame. Hopkins was a British Jesuit who knew John Henry Newman and, like Newman, converted to Roman Catholicism from the Church of England. He was studying theology in North Wales in December of 1875 when he read about the *Deutschland* tragedy in the newspaper. The ship ran aground in the Thames estuary in a snowstorm and five Franciscan nuns —

exiled from Germany by Bismarck's anti-Catholic Falk laws—were among those who perished. Dad's grandfather Wilhelm Schickel left Germany at about the same time. Perhaps he too felt the sting of the Falk Laws.

The newspaper stories of the *Deutschland* wreck (which included witness accounts of one of the nuns, upon seeing the end was near, calling on Christ to *come quickly*) touched Hopkins deeply—and caused him to return to writing poetry. He had abandoned it for some time, believing it to be inconsistent with his Jesuit vocation. During his walks Dad would sometimes recite passages from Hopkins poems:

> *... stirred for a bird ...*
> *... I caught this morning morning's minion, kingdom of daylights dauphin...*
> *...all this juice and all this joy...*

Dad and Susie especially love Hansen's depictions of nineteenth century Catholic life. Nuns in habits. Jesuits with birettas in groups of three walking along the road leaning into the wind.

"WHERE ARE WE IN THE STORY?" Dad asked

as I searched out my bookmark in the slim hardback.

"The five nuns are on the ship," I said. "They have just left Germany and are headed to England. Sister Norberta and Sister Barbara are walking on deck and talking with that blowhard businessman. He's trying to impress them with his knowledge of oceanography."

I started to read:

Sister Norberta had forgotten about the male fascination with facts. With insincerity, she noted, "What interesting arithmetic."

Sister Barbara elbowed her.

Carl Dietrich Meyer seemed not to notice. Tamping his pipe tobacco with the head of a roofing nail, he told them, "Well, I do count myself an intellectual as well as a businessman. Of course, an intellectual is what an overeducated man calls himself when he has no particular talents."

Sister Barbara charitably said, "But your talent for conversation is much in evidence."

"Is it? I'm glad."

"I'm chilly," Sister Norberta said.

Herr Meyer smiled. "Oh well, hurry in, then! We shall have other opportunities to chat and dispute on this long voyage."

Crossing through the hatchway with Sister Barbara, Sister Norberta risked the joke, "I have just had my vocation to chastity confirmed."

Dad laughed and laughed.

HOPKINS' POEMS, famous now, were largely unpublished and ignored during his lifetime. We read a section where Hopkins showed an early draft of *The Wreck of the Deutschland* to one of his Jesuit friends, and tried to explain what he was doing with *sprung rhythm*—later considered Hopkins' great literary accomplishment. His friend didn't get it at all, and both priests agreed that the poem would probably never be published.

"Why write it then?" asked the friend.

To which Hopkins responded, "Why pray?"

"Amazing!" Dad said.

AMAZING INDEED. "I'll see you at lunch," I said to Dad.

"What time will that be?" Dad asked.

"Noon," I said.   I'll have your glass of wine at 11:45.

"Who will be there?" he asked.

"Just you and I," I told him.

"That's right," he said, sounding slightly disappointed.

FACE TO FACE

I headed out. It was 11:00 and I had a lot to get done in the next 45 minutes.

Joseph Schickel

6. Lucy

Our dining room table was full for the feast of St. Lucy. Dad was in high spirits, but our dog, Lucy, was kept outside. My sister Joy and her ten-year-old daughter Eva, two of my bachelor brothers, Ben and Martin, and our friend Father Tony joined Susie and five guys for dinner.

Susie lit two candles on the Advent wreath as we sang and waited:

> *Long is our winter, dark is our night,*
> *O come set us free, O saving light*
> *Come set of free, O saving light*
> *O come dwell among us, O saving light*

It's a beautiful song, and the addition of two more good female voices (Joy and Eva) helped the mix. Chuck roast with gravy, green beans, and mashed potatoes were on the table. The high ceilings of our old house flickered with candlelight and reverberated with sound. Dad beamed, Father Tony smiled, and I said "Let us pray."

> *Bless us O Lord and these thy gifts*
> *Which we are about to receive from thy bounty*
> *Through Christ our Lord, Amen.*

Schickel that I am, I occasionally try to do too much with dinner prayers. In this case I thought it would be nice if we sang *Sancta Lucia*, for the feast, and since it was a really short song (two words) we should sing it several times. It started just fine; I led with my best Dean Martin Italino.

> *Sancta Lucia, Sancta Lucia!*

It started to get funky the second time through. Will imitated Bill Murray's lounge singer on Saturday Night Live. Not to be outdone, Tom crooned Sinatra doing it his way. A harmony flamed out. There was a human yip, then a dog yap, and then the sound of

Lucy's claws against the window at the end of the table. We all turned to Lucy. Her face was right up against the glass. She yipped louder and her eyes pleaded to be let inside.

"Don't let the dog in," said Dad in that classic loud voice of the hearing impaired.

I tried to finish out the song, but to no avail.

Father Tony, whose prayerful sense of propriety is deeply ingrained, attempted to disguise his laughter with a cough, a bad idea. He got out of kilter, and couldn't catch his breath, and started making sounds that are hard to describe, but got your attention.

"She knows …………..we're singing …………… about her," he gasped between breaths. When he was finally able to draw in a breath he emitted a tenor braying sound. We all lost it. Grace was over.

"Let Lucy in," cried Eva. "She wants to sing with us."

"No!" said Dad, who hears little, but somehow managed to hear that. "Don't let the dog in!" Dad never called Lucy by her name.

Lucy stayed outside, and we dug in. Wine and water glasses clinked, and plates filled up.

"Will, leave some mashed potatoes for the others," said Susie.

"How long have you had Lucy now?" asked Eva.

57

"About ten years," said Susie.

"Where did you get her?"

"From Father Tony," said Will. "Somebody dropped her off at the rectory when she was a puppy." He pointed out the picture on our bulletin board showing Tony, the three boys, and Lucy on the front porch the day he delivered her. Lucy had been a very cute puppy.

"She's a good watchdog," said Tom.

"How did you pick the name Lucy?" asked Eva.

"She has a white spot on her chest that reminded me of a light," said Susie. "The name Lucy comes from the word light."

"I have always loved the name Lucy," said Eva.

"Me too," said Susie.

"What's the dog's name?" asked Dad.

"Lucy," said Joy, who thankfully was sitting right next to him. She leaned over very close to his ear when she said it, slowly and clearly.

"Interesting," said Dad.

"What have you been reading lately, Grandpa," asked Eva.

"Well, Eva, my eyes are pretty bad and it's getting really hard for me to read," he said. "But Joe and Susie have been reading me a great book about the actor Sidney Poitier. Have you ever heard of him?"

"I don't think so," said Eva.

"Well he's a great actor," said Dad. "I think you would like him.

Dad, Susie and I had been reading Sidney Poitier's autobiography, *The Measure of a Man*. It tells the story of his journey from poverty on Cat Island in the Bahamas to Hollywood fame with hits like *To Sir with Love* and *In the Heat of the Night*. We were longtime fans of his movies—but knew little of the story of his life.

A few days earlier we had read the amazing story of his survival at childbirth. I fetched the book and read a short excerpt at the table.

Poitier's parents, who were very poor, were in Miami selling tomatoes when he was born, very prematurely, weighing less than three pounds. His father, who had already lost children to disease and stillbirth, was stoic. He went to the undertaker in the "colored" section of Miami and came back with a shoebox to serve as a casket.

But his mother had other ideas. She went to a local soothsayer. The two women held hands in silence for a long time. Then the soothsayer twitched, groaned, made gurgling sounds and said, "Don't worry about your son. He will survive and he will not be a sickly child.... He will travel to most of the corners of the earth. He will walk with kings. He will be rich and famous. Your name will be carried all over the world. You must not worry about that child."

"What an amazing story," said Joy.

"Amazing," said Eva.

WE SAT IN THE LIVING ROOM, drank coffee, and watched the first half of the movie *Lilies of the Field,* which won Sidney Poitier an Academy Award for Best Actor in 1964. I saw it as a child and it's a great movie. It's the story of a group of Catholic nuns who escaped Communist Berlin and came to the American Southwest, where they hoped to set up a school, hospital, and chapel. They hired Homer Smith, a black traveling handyman played by Poitier, to "Build us a ssschapel." The story centers on the relationship between the stony Mother Superior and Homer—who butt heads hard and often, but also grudgingly admire each other. The chapel gets built. The movie is perhaps best known for its classic scenes of Homer teaching a bunch of German nuns to sing the gospel song *Amen.*

"Homer Smith was a *helluva man,*" said Dad. We had stopped halfway through the movie. Dad was tired and said he wanted to go to his "roost pole."

"Roost pole?" asked Eva. "What's that?"

"It's where an old buzzard like me sleeps at night," said Dad.

It conjured quite an image, and Eva laughed. "Grandpa," she said, "Don't you think Mother Superior was a *helluva woman?*"

Now it was Dad's turn to laugh, and Joy joined in, looking proud.

"Yes she was, my dear," Dad said. "Homer more than met his match with that one."

We said night prayer in the living room. Goodnights and sleep wells were exchanged. Dad tapped his way into his room and closed the door.

MORNING	MID DAY	EVENING
PREPARE BREAKFAST	PREPARE LUNCH	PREPARE SUPPER
SET TABLE	SET TABLE	SET TABLE
CLEAR DINING AREA	CLEAR DINING AREA	CLEAR DINING AREA
PUT AWAY FOOD	PUT AWAY FOOD	PUT AWAY FOOD
WASH DISHES	WASH DISHES	WASH DISHES
SWEEP FLOOR	SWEEP FLOOR	SWEEP FLOOR

FOOD PREPARATION	HOUSE CLEANING	CLOTHING CARE
HARVESTING	STAIRS	FOLDING
PREPARE VEGETABLES	HALLWAYS	IRONING
BAKING	LIVING ROOM	WASHING
CHURN BUTTER	DINING ROOM	PUTTING AWAY
SHOPPING	BASEMENTS	SHEET LAUNDRY
DESERT	BATH ROOMS	

SPECIAL		CHILDREN
FLOWER ARRANGEMENT		GAMES
GIFT WRAPPING		READING
SEWING		WALKS
MUSIC		BABY

7. The Pegboard

Arrange it carefully and then dance like hell!
William Schickel

*I know, I know.   We are your chosen people.   But once in
a while, can't you choose somebody else?*
Tevye in *Fiddler on the Roof* by Joseph Stein

"If Grandpa moved into our house he would bring the Pegboard with him." said Tom. The world knew Dad as a modern artist, but his grandchildren knew him as the inventor of the Pegboard.

Our three sons were familiar with the Pegboard. I grew up on a small farm and Dad developed the Pegboard as a management device to assign chores among his eleven children. It was a 20" x 20" board that listed about fifty tasks that needed to be done on a regular basis—farm things like feeding cows, hauling manure, working in the garden—household things like fixing meals, cleaning, laundry etc. Each of us kids was assigned a color and several pegs. Each morning we had to check the Pegboard to see which chores we were responsible for. And my memory is that it worked pretty well. Although once one of my brothers stole it and buried it in a hole in the back yard. Mr. Goodie Two Shoes himself saved the day. I rescued the Pegboard and returned it to its proper place—and moral order was restored in Pickleville.

IT WAS EARLY MAY OF 2007, about a month after Mom died. Dad was still living in the old house by himself and getting eager to move out. Susie and I had invited Dad to live with us, but he was also seriously looking at some care facilities nearby. Susie and I were having a *family discussion* with the boys about the possibility of having Dad come live with us.

"What do you think?" Susie asked the boys.

"I think it would be fine," said Will.

"I think it would be a disaster," said Tom. "People already think we're like Amish people. Now they'll think we are an Amish nursing home."

"He wouldn't bring the Pegboard with him," I said.

Charlie was quiet.

"What do you think, Charlie," Susie said.

"I don't know," said Charlie. "It's hard to think what it would be like. Could I still bring my friends over?"

"It would be terrible," said Tom. "He'll bring that stupid Pegboard. He'll want us to pray all the time. We'll never get to watch TV."

"I think it would be fine," said Will. "I would like to get to know him better. He really needs help."

DAD LIKED TO HAVE A DAILY ROUTINE. And he would want *us* to have one if he lived with us. Pegboard spirituality was a basic tenet at the Church of What's Hap'nin' Now. Watch out!

He thought that having a daily routine gave him a tool to organize and arrange his life to make it happy and productive. In today's hectic world, he told me, if you don't have a routine you become overwhelmed and confused, and don't really know what you are doing or how you are spending your time. If you have a regular daily schedule or routine you can consciously arrange your day to include a fresh and lively mix of work, prayer, recreation, exercise, meals, sleep, social activities, intellectual pursuits, hobbies—you name it. Basically a daily routine lets you keep track of your life—and "fine tune" or adjust it—day by day, season by season, year by year. I never thought to ask him if a regular daily routine would get him (or me!) to heaven. But my guess is he would have said, "That depends on what's in the routine and how well you keep it."

Dad approached that amazing work of creation called *a day*—much as he approached a painting—particularly his combination graphic and drip paintings. These paintings have hard-edged graphic backgrounds—in serigraph, cut metal, enamel paint, etc. Onto this background he would then apply his free form drip paint, or some other material.

He would lay out the hard edged background slowly and analytically—often making adjustments or stopping and starting over a number of times until he got the background just the way he wanted it. This was the *work* part. Then he would switch psychological gears and begin the *play* part. The music in the shop would go from Bach to Monk—and sometimes he would take his shoes off. First he would practice his moves without paint a number of times. Then he would spontaneously pour, drip, and sometimes splatter paint onto the graphic surface. He identified strongly with jazz musicians who know the tonal and rhythmic structures of the piece so well that they are able to improvise—dancing up, down, around, in, out and through the piece—undulating with soulful abandon. It's intense and liberating. Exhausting and exhilarating. He never said this, but I thought a bit of the boxer came out in him when he was doing his bigger drip paintings. He moved like a fighter: stealthy, alert, light on his feet.

Dad thought that a day, a season, a year, a life, a musical composition, a painting, a sculpture, a house, a prison, a monastery, a resort, a church, a city, a life —to be considered human or religious or Christian in any *meaningful* way—must be equally infused with both hard-edged orthodoxy and the soulful orgasmic dance —like God's first testament—creation. Dad loved that idea of the first testament. In 1980 he gave the annual Dolle Lecture at Saint Meinrad Archabbey in Indiana, and the title was *The First Testament.*

"Arrange it carefully and then dance like hell!" was his advice for almost any project or endeavor. But unlike many moderns *he didn't skimp on that orthodox part*—as his children on a little farm in Pickleville were well aware—witness the Pegboard. And it was that orthodox part that had my three teenage boys worried when they thought about Grandpa coming to live with us!

The boys had seen the pictures and heard the stories about life on the farm when I was a kid. In Schickel lore the Pegboard was an iconic symbol of Germanic discipline, moral rectitude, orderliness, and goodness—long before Mom died and Dad came to live with us. The black and white pictures of life on the farm gave it an ancient, other worldly feel. My x-box generation sons found it interesting *only in small doses*. If I pushed Schickel traditions too hard I encountered stiff resistance.

"Could we still go on vacation?" asked Charlie.

"Yes," I responded. "My brother John said he would look after Grandpa when we were on vacation."

DAD AND I SPENT A LOT OF TIME TOGETHER on my non-firehouse days. We had a lot to talk about *before* Mom died. We were working on several ongoing projects related to his artwork and the William Schickel Gallery. Katharine Carter, our museum consultant, had a couple of museum exhibits in the works and we wanted to keep those moving ahead. A second edition of the book *Sacred Passion: the Art of William Schickel* by Gregory Wolfe was being published by the University of Notre Dame Press. There was a lot of photography and layout work related to this. Margot Patterson from the *National Catholic Reporter* was planning to visit in August for a feature story on Dad.

With Mom's death we now had to look after her estate, for which I was executor, and Dad's living situation. And as if that wasn't enough—Dad announced almost immediately that he intended to write a book about Mom. It would be called *What a Woman!* and it would be a tribute to his wife and lover of over sixty years. Dad's writing projects had been collaborations (with me) for many years now. I was thrilled to help him write a book about Mom. But I also knew it would be a lot of work — and my plate was pretty full. And Dad made it clear he did not want [me] to dilly-dally on this. He wanted the book out by Christmas!

Dad really loved Mom. That was obvious and he had good reason. Beautiful Mom, beautiful Mary!

Serene and bright! How could you not love her? Mom loved Dad too but that was a different matter. The reasons, how to put this, were not as obvious. Everybody loved Mom! Dad? He had a good circle of friends and acquaintances. A lot of people admired him. But he was harder to love than Mom, especially in his later years.

April moved into May and Dad wanted to get out of the big house. It was psychologically difficult to be in the home he had shared with Mom for so many years—without her. Mom was such an artful homemaker. The old house oozed her presence. To be there without her was very painful for Dad. It was like she was there, but she wasn't there.

He also had some very practical reasons to move out. He thought that having people come over several times each day to visit, fix or bring meals, clean, bring supplies etc.—was too much of a burden on his children. And he realized that getting up and down the stairs was becoming a real problem. His bedroom was upstairs, as was his workroom, which he and Mom had dubbed *Ora et Labora* (Latin for *Worship and Work)* He could still get up and down the stairs. But it was becoming very difficult and a huge worry. He was planning his day around getting up and down the stairs.

He and I started talking more seriously about living options. I brought him down to our house to look at possible room arrangements if he moved in with us. We started exploring and visiting care facilities in the area. Some of these were very nice and he had a pretty good reaction to them. By mid-May, Susie and I were thinking he would opt for a care facility.

We were still hopeful that Dad would accept our offer and move in with us. Naturally it was different for Susie than for me. She and Dad got along great. But they were not flesh and blood.

Susie had been primary caretaker for her Mom and Dad in their elder years. She had only one living brother, and he lived out of state. In the earlier years of our marriage her parents lived in Dayton, a little over an hour away. She drove up there with the boys on my firehouse days. It was exhausting. When her Mom died, we were not in a position to take her Dad into our home, and this caused her some regret and remorse. For dear loyal Susie, to take in my Dad would be part redemption, part guilt trip, and lots of hard work for an unknown period of time.

"GOOD MORNING DAD," I said. He was sitting

on his favorite couch downstairs in the old house. It was about 8:00 a.m. and I was just off work at the firehouse. As was now my usual pattern, I stopped by to spend time with Dad on the way home.

"Good morning Joe," he said. "How was your night?"

"Great," I said. "No runs after midnight."

"Looks like a beautiful day," he said.

"I've got some good Starbuck's coffee for you," I said, pouring some into the white mug he liked.

We chatted for a couple of minutes. I went into the kitchen and put out cereal and juice for breakfast. Then I went back and we did the scripture readings together. And then he popped the question.

"Joe, shortly after Mom died, you and Susie invited me to come and live at your house. Is that offer still good, or are you having second thoughts?" Dad asked.

"It's still good," I said.

"Well, then I would like to accept it," he said.

I was surprised, pleased, and relieved—and told him so. We had been visiting care facilities in the past couple of weeks and I was getting the idea that he might well opt for one of these.

Over breakfast we started talking about the timetable and work of making the move. He was eager to move as soon as possible, but recognized that we should get the work on his room done at our house (especially putting in the new bathroom) before he moved. Dad suggested moving in June and using the half bath in our hallway until his new bath was finished. I urged him against this. We targeted moving him in after our July vacation.

It dawned on me as I drove home that Dad's decision would be a surprise to Susie. She, like me, was expecting Dad to opt for a care facility at that point. I felt like Tevye in *Fiddler on the Roof* as he walked home to tell his wife Golde the *good news* that he had given permission for their eldest daughter Tzeitel to marry the impoverished tailor Motel.

She took it like a champ!

8. Making the Rounds

I was on a stepladder painting the ceiling of the William Schickel Gallery in downtown Loveland, about a quarter mile from our house, when my cell phone rang.

"Aslan is on the move," said Susie when I picked up.

"What?" I said, a little too sharply, coming out of the fog of my to do list. Since Dad had moved in, my patience with work interruptions had plummeted. It was often hard to find time to get basic tasks, like painting the damn gallery, done. Taking it out on dear loyal Susie? That was the work of a real man of genius!

"Dad is making the rounds, Bonehead" she said, laughing at my impatience.

"Sorry, I nearly fell off the ladder answering the phone," I said. Best excuse I could think of. "Where are you?"

"In the crows nest reading *Water for Elephants*," she said. "Dad is just getting on the bridge." When Dad moved in Susie had found an attic window which had a good view of much of downtown Loveland. When Dad was making the rounds she would perch herself up there, read, and keep an eye on Dad. She was a very lucky girl!

"Any bats up there?" I asked.

"I haven't seen any, but there are some droppings," she said. "Dad's headed for the gym. Can you check on him in a few minutes?"

"Got it," I said. "Talk to you later."

"Thank you," said Susie.

I descended the stepladder, walked down the stairs, and stood on the sidewalk. I looked to my right, and—there he came. He looked regal, part Henry VIII and part Dumbledor, descending the slope off the bridge. He sat erect in the green golf cart, grey beard and hair trailing in the wind, blue and gold Notre Dame cap perched atop his head. He was nice and warm and obviously enjoying himself. What a piece of work. Paragon of animals. Quintessence of dust. Yertle the friggin' turtle. King of the road. Master of mud!

Dad had been making the afternoon rounds in Loveland for as long as I could remember. There were always a few bars in the old part of town and Dad visited them all. In recent years it had been Cindy's or Paxton's. Before that it was the Whistle Stop, Friendly's, or the Harmony Inn. He usually only had one drink, and then returned to work. Making the afternoon rounds gave him daily contact with Loveland common folk, which he valued. With the men at the bar Dad was strictly a workingman. You could hear it in his voice—he talked like a hillbilly. With the women he would don or doff the mantle of *artiste* as a pragmatic matter. Some of the women found the *artiste* thing kind of charming.

By the time Mom died in 2007, downtown Loveland had a new exercise gym. Dad quickly became a member and going to the gym became the other part of his afternoon round making.

He turned left when he got off the bridge and disappeared behind a building. I walked to the end of the block and watched him pull up in front of the gym, parking as close to the door as possible. A white swipe key on a red lanyard was looped around his neck. With his cane he made it to the gym door, swiped his key, made his way inside and sat down.

I went back upstairs and worked for about fifteen minutes, then went down to visit Dad at the gym. I swiped my key and went inside. A woman in tights and sweats was doing cardio on the treadmill. A muscular man worked with dumbbells. Dad sat on the leg press machine at the far end of the room.

"Hi Dad," I called as I approached.

He peered up in my direction from under his cap, struggling to see who was talking to him.

"It's Joe," I said. "How are you doing?"

"Hey Joe," he said, "I'm doing great. What are you doing here?"

"I'm looking for Darien," I lied. "I have to talk to her about renewing my gym membership." Darien was one of the gym owners, and she did a great job of looking after Dad when he made the rounds.

"I haven't seen her." Dad said.

"I'm getting the gallery ready for Emil's show," I said. Dad's grandson Emil Robinson (www.EmilRobinson.com) is a successful young artist. He teaches drawing at the University of Cincinnati, is developing a good patron base, had a painting in the Smithsonian, and recently had a solo exhibit at

Waterhouse & Dodd in London. But this was a few years ago, and an exhibit of paintings was about to open at the William Schickel Gallery in Loveland, Ohio.

"How is Emil's exhibit coming along?" Dad asked.

"I don't have any paintings hung yet," I said. "I'm still painting the gallery. But I've seen most of them and it's going to look great."

"I can't wait to see it," said Dad. "Emil is very talented. Joe, could you adjust the weight to 60 lbs. for me?"

I moved the pin to 60 lbs. and he tried it.

"That's just right," he said, and proceeded to do ten leg presses.

"That ought to help your leg strength," I said.

"I sure hope so," he replied.

"Well, if you don't need me I'll get back to work." I said.

"I'm doing fine," he said. "And thanks for checking on me."

I LEFT THE GYM AND WALKED TWO BLOCKS to Cindy's Friendly Tavern. At the door I paused to let my eyes adjust to the light. Behind the bar, blond Cindy drew a tall glass of Budweiser from the tap, walked it down to the end of the bar, and placed it before her lone patron. She took two dollars from the wad on the bar in front of him, rang it into the cash register, and turned to me.

"What do you want, honey?" she asked.

"Dad will be by shortly," I said. "I wanted to make sure you still have my phone number in case he needs help."

"It's right here on the side of the cash register." she said. "I've got your number and your brother Martin's too. We'll keep a good eye on your Dad. I just love that man. What kind of artist is he anyway?"

"If you can figure that out you'll be doing better than most," I said.

"Hmmmmmmmmmmmm," said Cindy. "I've heard he's some kind of a modern artist.

"I really appreciate you keeping an eye on him," I said to Cindy.   "He loves coming here."

"Well we love having him," said Cindy. The man at the end of the bar nodded, affirming Cindy's statement. It was not in his pickled genes to disagree with Cindy.

I left the bar. As I walked back toward the gallery, I saw Dad's golf cart headed for Cindy's. I called Susie on the cell.

"Dad should be leaving Cindy's in about a half

hour," I told her.

"Got it," she said in Joespeak. She would monitor Dad's return journey from her crow's nest in the attic.

"I think you like reading up there," I said.

"I love reading with bats buzzing around my head," she said.

Point taken.

"I'll call you when he gets back," she said.

"Thank you." Flowers!!

I returned to painting the ceiling and thought about my family.

Six months earlier, the day after Mom's funeral, all eleven siblings had sat in our living room to address Dad's care. Among other things, we discussed the fact that Dad was still driving his car. It was dangerous and should stop. But ……..

"I vote against it," one of my siblings had said at the meeting.

*"*Vote!*?"* Susie said later when I told her about the siblings meeting. "What does voting have to do with anything! Who will actually tell him not to drive his car? Who will provide transportation*?"*

Dad's declining mobility and transportation needs were a growing and ever-present issue. In the two years he lived with us he went from car, to golf cart, to scooter. After the first year, we installed a wheelchair ramp outside his door, which was absolutely necessary at that point. I became a creative installer of railings and grab bars at our home and the William Schickel Gallery. Canes, walkers, wheelchairs, and exercise equipment including a stationary bicycle and inversion table cluttered the downstairs of our house. Dad was disciplined about getting exercise — at home, on his walks around the block, and at the gym.

Dad had to drive his golf cart for a short distance on the street when he made the rounds, and we were afraid the police would stop him. Loveland is very big on flowers along the streets, in parks, and downtown. There is a large and well-organized volunteer effort to plant and maintain the flowers. Dad's golf cart had a large utility box on back. I put gardening tools, fertilizer, and a big green watering can in the box.

"Taking care of the flowers!" was the standard line if anyone, and particularly the police, questioned him.

I was back up on the stepladder painting when my cell phone rang again.

"Dad's back home again," Susie said. "I just thought you would want to know. I've got piano students from 3:30-6:30 so I'll be leaving in a few minutes. There's pork roast in the crock pot."

"I'll come home shortly," I said.

WE WERE SHIFTING INTO AFTER-SCHOOL MODE. Tom and Charlie were already home. Will would get home about 5:00, after football. I went home to be with Dad and the boys while Susie taught until about 6:30. I would finish up the supper Susie had started and we would eat at 7:00 when Susie got back.

"DAD, YOUR ROOM IS VIBRATING," I said as I entered. Dad was sitting at his work table. My younger brother Benedict, who lived nearby, sat on a stool next to him.

"It's Tom playing keyboard upstairs," Ben said.

"It doesn't bother me a bit," said Dad. "I like it."

My son Tom's room was directly above Dad's. He had played the downstairs piano loud which irritated his brothers. So we bought him a keyboard with headphones and put it in his bedroom. When he wore the headphones you couldn't hear the music at all. However, you could clearly feel, in the room below him, the rhythm of Tom pounding the keys. Tom was a pounder of the first order.

"How is Tom's album coming," Ben asked.

"Behind schedule, but well," I said. Tom, age sixteen, was recording an album of seven original songs. It would be hard to overstate my pride in his talent and effort.

"Joe, I want you to take a look at Ben's new painting," Dad said. I moved behind Dad to have a look.

"The paint is still wet," Ben said. Dad held the painting under his work light. Ben is good at abstract composition and has an outstanding sense of color. It was a cool painting.

"You've got real talent, Ben." Dad said. "You do things that can't be taught. We should sell these at the William Schickel Gallery. "

DAD WAS ONE OF BEN'S BIGGEST FANS. It always pleased Dad to see Ben painting. Dad believed in Ben's talent, and encouraged him to be more regular, productive, and goal oriented about his painting.

"Try to do two paintings per week," Dad said. "Paint two hours every day."

"Should we list painting as a chore on the Pegboard?" I asked. Ben laughed and Dad didn't hear me.

"I like your idea of doing a painting together,"

Ben said to Dad. This was obviously something they had been discussing before I came in the room.

"I've never done it before, but I think it would really be fun," said Dad.

"Let's do it!" said Ben excitedly, and they sealed the deal with a handshake.

9. Band of Brothers

We few, we happy few, we band of brothers;
For he to-day that sheds his blood with me
Shall be my brother; be he ne'er so vile,
This day shall gentle his condition;
And gentlemen in England now-a-bed
Shall think themselves accurs'd they were not here,
And hold their manhoods cheap whiles any speaks
That fought with us upon Saint Crispin's day.

William Shakespeare
Henry V, Hal at Agincourt

FACE TO FACE

Never trust the person who tells you what you should do,
because only you know what you should do.
Yves R. Simon, Philosoper
University of Notre Dame

In the clearing stands a boxer, he's a fighter by his trade...
Paul Simon

It was a beautiful Friday night, about a half hour before game time, and Tiger Stadium behind Loveland High School pulsated with life. On the field the McNicholas Rocket and Loveland Tiger football squads went through pregame drills. The marching band played, cheerleaders waved pom-poms, and booster parents hawked concessions and split-the-pot tickets. And we, the loud, the proud, the many, the Loveland football faithful, in our scruffy splendor and gap-tooth glory, filled the stands wearing orange and black.

Hope was in the air! It was the second game of the season. Despite losing the first game of the season to a strong Turpin team, by the improbable score of 5-3, the Tigers were upbeat. They had been through several down years, but had an excellent new coach, lots of enthusiasm, and some pretty good, if yet unproved, talent. They had almost won the Turpin game. McNick had defeated Loveland for the past several years, but tonight the Loveland team saw an opportunity to break out of the past, set the course for a successful season.

"IT'S A BIG GAME," said Dad, as Susie and I wheeled him up the path to the stadium. "Will is starting, isn't he?"

"Yes. He's starting at defensive tackle," I said. I could hardly believe it myself. I had been lukewarm on Will's decision to play football his junior year, after not playing as a freshman or sophomore. I had gone to football superpower Moeller (I did not play football) where it was unthinkable to begin football your junior year, unless you were a transfer or superstar, which Will was not. Will's junior football season was tough, his success was limited. I was thrilled, and a bit surprised, when he won a starting spot his senior year. A good game tonight would mean a lot to Will and the Tigers.

Will and Dad connected over football. They would sit together on the porch, or in Dad's room, and talk about it.

"Boxing saved me in high school," Dad had told

him.

"I'm so glad I found football," Will replied.

Dad was enthusiastic about Will's decision to play football when I was still skeptical. In retrospect, it is clear that Will found something deeply satisfying in football.

THE LOVELAND FIGHT SONG FILLED THE AIR as the team passed in front of us, cleats clacking on tarmac, headed for the locker rooms for final instructions from coaches. At 5'8" Will's helmet barely poked above the shoulder pads of taller players. "I hope he does well," said Dad from beneath his Tiger ball-cap. "That boy sure loves football."

The cop guarding the gate onto the field noted Dad's wheelchair and allowed him to take his usual spot on the track just inside the fence. Susie and I set up lawn chairs beside him.

Dad really liked it there because he felt close to the action. The fact that it was difficult to see the game (sideline players, band members, cheerleaders and photographers often blocked the view) was not a problem for Dad. He couldn't see that far anyway. What he liked was the feeling of being in the middle of things. Players, cheerleaders, and band were close and he could hear them. People standing at the fence behind him could come up and talk with him. It worked well.

The game started poorly, with McNick quickly scoring two touchdowns and taking a 14-0 lead. But by halftime Loveland had tied the score at 14-14. Dad was getting cold and tired. Susie took him home and I watched the second half from the stands, where you could actually see the game.

In the fourth quarter Dad called on my cell phone.

"I tried to go to sleep but I couldn't," he said. "What's the score?"

"It's tied at 21-21," I said. "There's only two minutes to go."

"Who has the ball?" he asked.

"Loveland," I said. "We're driving down the field." I stopped talking for a minute to watch the play. "Dammit we just got intercepted. I'll call you back."

"What's happening now …..!?" I could hear him asking as I dumped the call to watch the game.

McNick had just intercepted the ball at their own 15 yard line. The Loveland drive had been stopped. The raucous Loveland fans fell silent, as the Tiger defense took the field.

On the first play from scrimmage after the

interception, Will somehow got into the McNick backfield and met the tailback just as he took the handoff. Somebody yelled "fumble!" and I saw a loose ball. There was a huge pileup in the McNick backfield at the 10 yard line. Refs pulled bodies off the pile and found Will at the bottom with the ball. He handed it to the ref. The Loveland faithful howled approval as the offense retook the field. A few plays later Loveland scored the game-winning touchdown. The final score was 28-21.

THE VICTORY WAS SWEET. Clouds of steam rose into the cool night air above bloodied, shirtless players, who crowded around grills behind the high school for their post game meal. Dads with spatulas scrambled to distribute cheeseburgers and water. Players laughed and cajoled as coaches offered congratulations. A jubilant Will took rib shots and chest bumps from his very good friends—his band of brothers—then sat on the blacktop to inhale cheeseburgers and savor the moment.

William Ryan Florian Schickel cast off a family curse that night. He came from a line of skinny farm boys who had avoided the gridiron with good reason. His athletic achievement there was un-precedented in my family. As the season progressed, and victories mounted, I heard many times from parents and coaches that Will was the "heart of the team"—a statement which never failed to make this once-skinny farm boy swoon with pride and admiration.

The unbiased author believes that the season turnaround can be traced to *that exact moment* when one of the smallest defensive tackles in the FAVC meat-hooked, flayed, filleted, splayed, waylaid, and took the ball *away*—from a McNick tailback. And be warned...I like to show the videotape!

ON A RAINY FRIDAY NIGHT TWO MONTHS LATER, in the last game of that season, Loveland's first winning season in eight years, Loveland upset rival Milford on a very muddy field. Proud parents watched the postgame celebration. The seniors rang the victory bell, huddled with their coaches, dove in the mud, posed for pictures, then lined up together at the edge of the field, and stepped off together. It was a cool moment, and I noticed Will's little brother Charlie, then in seventh grade, watching with intense interest and obvious admiration. Charlie's football fire was kindled that night. And since that remarkable season, the *Will Schickel Band of Brothers Award* has been given out each year at Loveland High School to a football player who overcomes adversity and makes unusual contributions to team spirit.

William Schickel, boxer, circa 1940

10. Notre Dame

There's blood in the bricks.
Frank O'Malley of Notre Dame

The Catholic College, as a College of Christ, should be a community of students and teachers centered in Christ....[T]he marrow of a Catholic College is not a system of thought, but a saving personality.
Frank O'Malley

"Dad, it says here that Notre Dame was a little

Catholic boarding school in the middle of nowhere back in your day." I was reading from a brochure while Susie pushed Dad's wheel chair across campus.

"That's true," Dad said. "And kind of appropriate, don't you think?"

"Absolutely," I replied.

"It sure has changed," Susie said.

It was a beautiful fall afternoon on the majestic campus of the University of Notre Dame. Notre Dame. Madre de Jesus. His Mother but Our Lady. *Notre* Dame. The American University named for the Mother has much in common with the Son's Roman Church. Both have humble origins in backwater locations. Both are awe inspiring in their tireless and enthusiastic pursuit of the good, the true, and the beautiful. Both achieved remarkable success, and became magnets for big ambition and its loyal sidekick—grand scale human failings. Both are institutionally conflicted about their plucky, embattled bastions of male dominance. Interestingly, those battlements are fairly often manned—or rather defended—by women. Notre *Dame*.

The Catholic Church and Notre Dame both love the pageantry, icons, and often cheesy trappings of traditional Christianity. In a television age this makes them uniquely vulnerable when their human failings become news. If you were an ambitious television reporter, would you pass up the opportunity to deliver your major scandal story with the Golden Dome or the Bernini Colonnade in the background?

"Dad, are there any gargoyles on the Notre Dame campus?" I asked.

"I think there are some at Alumni Hall," he replied.

"Maybe they could use a few more," I said.

"Interesting thought," he said.

Dad liked gargoyles and steeples together. Steeples represent human aspiration for the divine. Gargoyles depict God thumbing his nose at our actual performance. He smiled broadly as Susie and I pushed his wheelchair past the Basilica of the Sacred Heart and around the main building with its glorious Golden Dome.

"Gene Jaeger and I used to live in that building," said Dad. "I had some great times here. I hated high school but loved college."

We came to the Presbytery building. It was a beautiful part of campus and we walked slowly, letting the place sink in, the moment ripen.

"You and Norbert (his brother, my uncle, who also attended Notre Dame) were tight in college, weren't you?" I aked.

"Very close," he replied.

"Are those the bricks with the blood?" I asked, indicating the Presbytery. "Blood in the bricks," was a favorite phrase of Notre Dame's legendary English Professor Frank O'Malley.

"Yes," he said. "Great bricks, aren't they?"

"They tried to match these bricks in the new buildings," I said.

"Yes they did," Dad said. "And they got everything right except the most important thing."

This was the old part of campus that Dad knew, loved, and painted in his younger days. And it was just a stone's throw from here that he got his first art commission, at the Grotto.

We came upon the Grotto, and stopped at the edge to drink it in. Golden sun sparkled on St. Mary's Lake, filtered through orange and yellow leaves, and dappled the pavement. Students, staff, and visitors came and went. A serious looking, bearded student in jeans, leather jacket, and backpack knelt at the railing with head down. Female basketball players drank thirstily from the fountain, lit candles, knelt and prayed briefly. Cross-country runners paused for quick drinks, then ran on.

The Grotto. Cave of Candles. Place of Prayer and Miracles. It was built to replicate the Grotto at

Lourdes where Bernadette, at Mary's behest, scratched the ground and uncovered a spring that feeds the pool of water where countless numbers of pilgrims have experienced healing and other miracles. *Irish* legend has it that when this Grotto was moved to its current location on the Notre Dame campus, an underground spring was struck during construction, and that spring feeds the sculpted drinking fountain called *Living Water* that was *my* Dad's first art commission.

It's a beautiful fountain (no bias here) of cast and sculpted terrazzo, with three drinking spouts, and three Biblical images of Christ that pertain to water: *Calming the Storm*, *Washing the Apostles Feet*, and *Samaritan Woman at the Well*.

"It's a great spot," Dad said.

"*So* beautiful," said Susie.

We wheeled Dad up to the fountain. Water gurgled from the three spigots. Hispanic women who looked to be University housekeeping or kitchen staff, knelt at the railing. Dad leaned forward in his wheelchair and ran his hand along the terrazzo of the fountain.

"Looks good," he said. "It's been there over sixty years." He looked up at me and motioned for me to come closer. "How does it really look?" he whispered.

"It looks *wonderful*, Dad," Susie interjected. "And it's an honor to come here with you—and your nitwit of a son."

"Thank you sweetheart," I said. "You're my Wild Irish Petunia!"

"More like your Crazy German Brunhilde!" said Susie—eyes wide.

Dad laughed. A Notre Dame student guiding a group of visitors around campus overheard our conversation, and asked me if Dad was the artist who had done the fountain. I told her yes, and she made an announcement to the group, who offered applause, congratulations, and shouts of "Go Irish." The little man in the wheelchair sporting a black ball-cap grinned and pumped his fist in the air to the delight of the visitors. It was a cool moment for a man who had taken his lumps, figurative and literal, on the Notre Dame campus.

THAT CERTAINLY WAS A LONG SENTENCE," said Susie cheerfully. The tweedy philosophy professor seated to her right at the banquet for the annual meeting of the American Maritain Association had strung together a long sequence of large words during their introduction. He laughed at insouciant Susie and they got along great. We seated Dad near the podium, then I excused myself to check out the handicapped bathroom logistics. It was an older building and I suspected they might be difficult, which they were, but fortunately we made it through the evening without needing them.

Dr. David Solomon, from the University of Notre Dame Center for Ethics and Culture did a great job introducing Dad and presenting the award. Dad's comments were brief. He told the audience that he wasn't wearing the ball-cap to be cool, he needed it to protect his eyes from the light.

"We think it's cool anyway," a friendly voice called.

Two young culture vultures, one in Roman collar, schemed quietly on the perimeter.

"Who is he?" I overheard the one say.

"He helped Thomas Merton ruin Gethsemani," said the priest, just loud enough for me to hear.

Looking at pictures of the event a year later, Susie and I were struck at how good Dad looked, standing erect and smiling at the podium.

WE WERE BACK AT OUR ROOM at the Morris Inn.

"Joe," Dad called softly. I didn't respond, hoping

he would go back to sleep. Susie was sleeping next to me.

"Joe," he repeated, just a little louder. I slipped out of bed and sat on the floor next to his bed.

"What is it Dad," I said.

"What time is it?" Dad asked.

"One o'clock," I said.

"I can't sleep," he said. "Could I have another Temazapam."

"Sure, Dad," I said. I handed him the tablet, then a glass of water.

"Thanks Joe," he said. "I am really enjoying the trip, but I'll look forward to getting back in my own room. This bed is really high."

"I'm afraid you will fall out," I said.

"It was a great evening," Dad said. "It was great to see Tony and Judy Simon again." Tony Simon is the son of the philosopher Yves R. Simon, who was Dad's teacher and friend at Notre Dame.

"Nobody even cussed you out," I said. "Kind of unusual."

Dad laughed.

"That's one advantage of being old and hard of hearing," he said. "Most of the time I can't hear them cussing at me. They could blacklist me again and I wouldn't even know it!"

TEN YEARS EARLIER Dad, Mom, and I had attended another conference at Notre Dame. Dad's artwork was exhibited and he gave a talk. The "culture wars" were at fever pitch. Dad and his art were lightning rods. Dad and *Mom* were publicly sworn at and mocked by the holy rollers. A black-robed Benedictine publicly urged the faithful to take Dad's evil paintings off the walls and out to the dumpster. After the conference, one of the organizers (a "culture warrior" of the first rank) sought me out and apologized for the swearing on behalf of the conference and the University. "That guy isn't wrapped very tight," he confided to me about his raging lunatic sidekick. I responded that his gang had openly encouraged prejudice against contemporary art. To now apologize when somebody took it a little further than he liked, seemed phony.

"So you think it's stopped?" I asked Dad.

"I don't wanna know," he said.

Outside student revelers sang "Sweet Mollie Malone" as discordantly as possible. Susie woke and listened in.

"It bothered me but I think it bothered Mary a lot more," Dad said. "She just couldn't understand it. I think that was the last time she visited Notre Dame."

"No, she came back later when you received the Lauck Award," Susie explained.

"That's good," he said. "I'm glad her last visit here was better."

"They saw the devil and it was me," laughed Dad.

"You tried to fool them but you couldn't," I said. "They were onto you. Should we read a little *Exiles*?

"I'd like that," he said.

I found the book and read a stanza from the poem *Wreck of the Deutschland.*

> *Thou mastering me*
> *God! Giver of breath and bread;*
> *World's strand, sway of the sea;*
> *Lord of living and dead;*
> *Thou has bound bones and veins in me, fastened me flesh,*
> *And after it almost unmade, what with dread,*
> *Thy doing; and dost thou touch me afresh?*
> *Over again I feel thy finger and find thee.*

Dad grunted with deep satisfaction. "Amazing," he said. "Would you mind reading it again?"

I read it again, he grunted after every line.

"Incredible," he said. "I can see Frank O'Malley reading that from his classroom podium like it was yesterday. He read it twice. The room was silent, enthralled. He stood at the podium for several minutes with his eyes closed. I think he was praying. Then he picked up his notes, quietly left the room, and walked down the hall to his office. Class was over. You could have heard a pin drop."

"Wow," I said … at a loss for words. Silence would have been more appropriate.

"It hit me like a ton of bricks," Dad said. "I never recovered."

"Was there blood in those bricks?" I asked.

"Yes, and after they hit me there was blood *on* the bricks," he replied.

"Maybe that's why you lost your last round in the Bengal Bouts," I said. "You were standing there in the ring thinking about poetry and Sam Dolce cold-cocked you." The Bengal Bouts is a popular boxing tournament at Notre Dame which raises money for the Holy Cross Missions in Bengal. In his freshman year Dad won his early rounds in the tournament, but lost in the final round to defending bantamweight champ, Sam Dolce.

"I've been cold cocked plenty of times," said Dad, "and usually it was a good thing."

"Can't we get some sleep?" said Susie, laughing. "Is this ever going to end?"

"Oh, I'm sorry Susie, did we wake you?" said Dad.

"It's okay," she said. "I enjoyed hearing the conversation."

"Should I read a little more?" I asked.

"I'd like that."

I read a section about two priests, a Dominican and a Jesuit, who both smoked while reading their breviaries outside together. The Dominican felt scruples about the propriety of this and suggested consulting their superiors. The next day the Dominican was surprised to see that the Jesuit was still smoking. The Jesuit asked the Dominican how he had put the question to his Superior. "Am I permitted to smoke while I am praying?" said the Dominican. The Jesuit took a drag and said nothing. So the Dominican asked the Jesuit how he had framed the question. The Jesuit replied, "Am I permitted to pray while I'm smoking?"

Dad laughed and laughed.

"Well I hope we can all sleep now," I said, suddenly sleepy again. It was 2:30.

We said our *good nights* and *sleep wells*.

And got about four hours sleep.

IT WAS EARLY SUNDAY AFTERNOON AND

WE WERE DRIVING HOME. We left the Golden Dome behind—passed the factories, smokestacks, and bars of hardscrabble South Bend — and entered the flat open country of north central Indiana.

Dad rode shotgun and I drove. Susie rode in back, leaned up between the two front seats, and read to us from a new book called *Will in the World* by Steven Greenblatt. It's about William Shakespeare and his family living in Elizabethan England. She was reading from a chapter called *The Great Fear*, which focused on the fear of recusant (secret) Catholics in the time of Elizabeth. Engrossing stuff for a Catholic Anglophile literary wannabee, who had just breathed in the rarified academic air of a major university. Outside our van the small town Indiana of John Mellekamp's *Ain't That America* flew by. But inside we plumbed the murky, viscous waters of Tudor religious conflict. With luck we could make home *without a bathroom break*. I put the hammer down.

IN THE 1520'S HENRY VIII fiercely attacked Luther and was rewarded by the Pope with the title Defender of the Faith. England was universally Catholic. But in 1533 Henry, wanting a divorce and the wealth of the monasteries, declared himself Supreme Head of the Church in England and banned

Catholicism. There were many martyrs, including Thomas More and John Fisher.

In 1553 England became officially Catholic again when Mary Tudor assumed the throne. But Mary died childless in 1558 (six years before William Shakespeare's birth in 1564) and she was succeeded by protestant Elizabeth, who banned the practice of Catholicism again. The penalties were severe, including loss of prestige, property, and employment; also torture and execution.

Once again there were many recusants (secret Catholics) including William Shakespeare's mother, and perhaps other members of his family. The brilliant and high-profile Catholic scholar Edmund Campion, like many seriously religious folks, tried hard to live in both camps, inwardly Catholic and outwardly Protestant. Elizabeth liked and admired Campion and sought to work with him within limits. But in 1572 (Shakespeare was eight) Campion fled across the water to Douai in present day France. Douai, with its Catholic seminary, was a safe haven for English Catholics in exile. Campion became a Jesuit, returned to England as clandestine missionary and was eventually martyred. In 1575 a much lesser known scholar named Simon Hunt (who was Shakepeare's teacher from ages seven to eleven, from

1571-1575) also fled for Douai and became a Jesuit. It is entirely possible (but impossible to prove) that William Shakespeare met, knew, or even studied under Edmund Campion.

"There are martyrs today," said Susie. "Look at Sister Dorothy Stang."

The American Catholic missionary Sr. Dorothy Stang, SND de Namur was martyred in 2005 in Brazil for her work on behalf of the poor and indigenous peoples of the Amazon basin. Susie had known Sister Dorothy and her family growing up at St. Rita Parish in Dayton, Ohio.

"It's amazing how little has been asked of me for my faith," Dad said.

"But you've given a lot for your faith, Dad," Susie said.

"I don't think so," Dad said. "I've been a lucky son of a gun. I've had it easy." I glanced over my shoulder at Susie who smiled at me and shook her head.

"You're an interesting son of a gun," she said to Dad.

"I'm a lucky old buzzard who's looking forward to getting home and heading for the roost pole," he said. "What is that screeching sound?"

Dad, who is very hard of hearing, was the first to

hear the siren. The speeding ticket is hard to read, the humorless Indiana cop seemed to be writing with a blunt instrument. I am pretty sure the ticket says 92 miles per hour, but Susie insists it says 94 miles per hour.

"I didn't say anything!" said Susie breaking the long silence that filled our van after we got back on the road, at a careful, slow, and legal rate of speed.

I fiddled with the radio as darkness fell.

"Joe, I hate to tell you this, but I really need to go to the bathroom."

How little is asked of us.

Joseph Schickel

11. Where the River Bends

Hello Ohio
The back roads
I know Ohio
Like the back of my hand
Alone Ohio
Where the river bends
And it's strange to see your story end

From the song *Ohio*, by the musical group
Over The Rhine. Words and music by Linford Detweiler
and Karin Bergquist

FACE TO FACE

She was beauty, but when she came to me,
She must have thought I'd lost my mind.

From the song *Lucille* by Kenny Rogers

Just upriver from Cincinnati, the broad Ohio makes a lazy turn. On its north bank, called *the Yankee side* by my brother, Kentucky State Senator John Schickel, there is a fine amphitheater called Riverbend. It's the biggest outdoor music venue in the area, with seating capacity of over twenty thousand. The Cincinnati Symphony Orchestra and popular acts like Jimmy Buffet, Neil Young, Dire Straits and the Grateful Dead appear regularly. In 2008, Riverbend opened a new, smaller amphitheater right next to the big one, for smaller concerts. It's called PNC Pavillion and the first group to perform there, on April 8, 2008, was the Cincinnati group Over The Rhine. Susie and five guys got tickets.

IT WAS A WARM SPRING EVENING. Will wheeled Dad to his seat, steadied his transfer, and found a place to stow the wheelchair. Susie returned from the concession stand with a cardboard carrier of drinks. The boys took their sodas and walked down to check out the stage. Susie and I sat with Dad, sipped beer, and watched the place fill up. Dad sipped red wine. He looked relaxed and satisfied.

"We should have brought the coffee can," he said casually.

Susie blanched and I groaned, inwardly, I like to think. Dad was apparently receiving a message, hopefully not yet urgent, from Bladder Command. The coffee can, the damn *coffee can*, was Dad's urine receptacle of choice at home. He kept it near his bed or work table, and if the effort of getting to the bathroom (or later the potty chair) was too much, he opted for the coffee can. He preferred it over the plastic portable urinals we tried because he was better able to *hear his progress*. This particular coffee can gave a satisfying tinny ring, like rain on a metal roof but with a higher pitch, when he hit his mark. If the house was quiet you could hear it in the next room. The idea that Dad would consider peeing right in the middle of PNC Pavillion was not really a surprise to us. More about this shortly. But for now, I knew I had to act quickly.

"Let's go to the restrooms now," I said to Dad, "before the concert begins." If he had time to ponder his situation, he might opt for finishing his wine and then peeing in his cup.

"I can wait a while," said Dad.

"Better to do it now," Susie urged. She looked grim. Thankfully he agreed to go.

Taking Dad to a public restroom in his wheelchair was never easy. But fortunately Riverbend had good handicapped facilities. Things went smoothly, and we were back in our seats before the concert began.

IT WAS A WONDERFUL CONCERT, and they played a good number of the songs we knew. Dad couldn't see the stage very well, but fortunately there was a jumbotron near us, which he watched intently.

Karin Berquist and Linford Dettweiler are the two mainstays of the group. Karin sings most of the leads, with Linford doing keyboard or guitar and backup vocals. As a performing couple, they are a bit like Sonny and Cher—a big voiced gorgeous woman fronting her smirking composer husband.

Karin is a wonderful singer and natural performer. She has a rich bluesy voice. Also a good figure, blonde hair, graceful movements, and an easy presence. She's a beauty, and her face on the jumbotron was obviously launching Dad's ship. He moved his head slightly to the music, and was utterly enthralled as the band launched into *Jesus in New Orleans*, a song we knew pretty well.

The last time I saw Jesus,
I was drinking bloody Mary's in the South
In a barroom in New Orleans,
rinsin' out a bad taste in my mouth

The old man in the crusty ball cap was positively transfixed — and the band played on.

She wore a dark and faded blazer,
With a little bit of lining hanging out
When the jukebox played Miss Dorothy Moore
I knew that it was him without a doubt.

"Was Grandpa praying to the jumbotron?" Tom whispered to me during the applause after the song.

"I think he was praying to what he saw on the jumbotron," I whispered back.

Blank stare from Tom.

"Worshiping a beautiful woman," I elaborated. "He's been doing it most of his life."

Incredulous stare from Tom. Smirk back from me.

"Are you're telling me that Grandpa is a pagan?" asked Tom.

"Only half," I said. Tom rolled his eyes, and OTR launched into their next song.

TOWARD THE END OF THE CONCERT Dad got cold so we left a little early. Actually we were all ready to go. It had been a great outing. I cranked up the heater in the van, Dad fell asleep, and we headed back to Loveland.

ABOUT A YEAR AFTER DAD DIED, Susie and Tom met OTR's Karin Bergquist and Linford Detweiler at a songwriting workshop in Santa Fe, and they had some great conversations. Karin and Linford, it turned out, were regular visitors to Gethsemani (where they sometimes went to do songwriting) and admirers of Dad's work. Tom and Susie were able to tell them how much Dad had enjoyed their music, that it had been a comfort to him in his old age, and how transported he had been at their Riverbend concert.

UPON READING AN EARLY DRAFT OF THIS CHAPTER, Susie impressed upon me that Dad's uniquely casual attitude about public urination was a subject that should really not go uncelebrated in this book. And so we return to a topic briefly touched upon earlier. For Dad, if you were outside and a male, urination was a simple matter and no big deal. We leave it to generations and art historians hence to ponder whether this predilection, which became pronounced in his later years, stems from country living, pride of endowment, the creative urge, the desire to embarrass one's young—or something else.

The man would pee in parking lots, at football games, out the car door—in traffic! A block from City Hall in downtown Cincinnati he mentioned to me that he was starting to feel the urge.

"I'm sure there are restrooms in City Hall," I said, but too late. Already he was making his way, unzippingly, to the wall of the historic Isaac Wise Temple, calmly leaving his mark. I pulled my cap down over my face and prayed that Engine 14 wouldn't come rolling around the corner. One more setback for Cincinnati's ecumenical movement!

In the parking lot of LaRosa's Restaurant in Loveland, Dad, ever the gentleman and wishing to spare the tender sensibilities of dear Susie who had just taken him to lunch, discretely turned away from her before unzipping and letting fly. *Unfortunately*, his shift of position put him in full view of a bustling lunch crowd through the plate glass window. *Fortunately* this took place *after* they had eaten. Otherwise Susie would have had the memorable privilege of pushing this minor celebrity through the

LaRosa's lunch crowd after the event. Doubtless friends and neighbors would have wanted to congratulate him on his good show!

"Bertha, what's the name of that artist who lives in Loveland?
"I think it's Skenkle, or Shinkel or something like that.
"I think he just peed on our rose bushes!"
I wake in a cold sweat.

My siblings can contribute many more stories to fill this literary niche. My goal is not an exhaustive treatment of the subject. Rather, at Susie's urging, I simply wish to "open the discussion" and "raise awareness" regarding this nascent issue. Susie's fear, I believe, is that I have inherited my Dad's condition, which will become more pronounced in my later years. If she can spare even one child or grandchild the associated filial mortification—her efforts will not have been in vain.

Fat chance!

Joseph Schickel

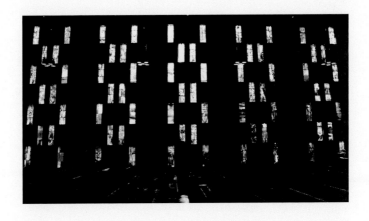

12. Sunday

The Spirit comes to the aid of our weakness; for we do not know how to pray as we ought, but the Spirit himself intercedes with **inexpressible groanings**.

Romans 8:26

The morning sun filtered through lush green leaves and sparkled on river rapids on the Little Miami as our minivan ambled out of town on Riverside Avenue. It was a morning crisp and cool, but the afternoon would be hot.

Our van was dusty and red. The wipers had come to rest in the "up" position. The left taillight assembly was messed up. Happily, the air conditioner worked, though many other electronics, including some of the window controls, did not. A grey bearded, stoop shouldered, ball-cap pated, elder statesman was riding shotgun. His grey haired, stoop shouldered, grim faced, four-eyed son was driving. Three teenage boys with "when will it be over" looks rode in back.

It was 9:00 a.m. Dad, the boys, and I were driving to mass at St. Gertrude Church in Madeira. Susie had left the house much earlier. She was doing music at the 8:00 and 9:45 masses at St. Veronica. Dad and I liked to "check out" other parishes from time to time, and St. Gertrude had beautiful stained glass windows done by my grandfather, Emil Frei, Dad's artistic mentor and father-in-law. It was also a good place to hear the latest from the traditionalist wing (*Crisis, First Things, National Catholic Register*) of the church.

"Dad, what's all this silliness about *inexpressible groanings* in the readings? It doesn't sound very religious to me," I said. We had done scripture readings earlier over coffee.

"You'd think they could talk about chalices or praying or something holy," Dad chuckled.

"Speaking of groaning," I said. "Do you remember Dewey Alsop's funeral."

"Remind me of it," he said.

SO I TOLD HIM THE STORY. Dewey Alsop was the husband of Alma Alsop, an African American woman from Loveland who sometimes worked for my parents. We loved her dearly. Despite growing up poor in the thirties and forties in a small town that was psychologically if not geographically south of the Mason Dixon line, there was not an ounce of bitterness in her. She was one of those amazing people whose deep faith and sweet disposition allow them to rise above the many difficulties of their lives.

Alma always spoke lovingly of her husband, Dewey, who was an excellent stonemason. But we knew that Dewey's alcoholism, and related troubles, were heavy burdens for Alma. When Dewey died, I went to the funeral with Mom and Dad and some of my brothers and sisters at the First Baptist Church in Loveland.

As a youngster, I went to a number of funerals at Loveland's African American churches. It was memorable and formative. After one such service, Dad commented to me that we Catholics could learn much from these congregations about praying in general and the biblical concept of *spiritual intervention through inexpressible groanings* in particular. There was soulful serious groaning at those funerals, and the spirit's presence was palpable. You could see it in faces and hear it in the voices, though not always in words.

There were only a few whites at Dewey's funeral, in the little frame church at the corner of Chestnut and Main, a block from the small stone house Dewey built with his own hands, shortly after he and Alma were married. Fortunately, I was dressed up, because I remember being struck by how dignified the congregation looked, the men in dark suits, crisp white shirts and ties, the women in dark dresses and hats .

The minister had a voice like Paul Robeson. There was beautiful singing and soulful preaching, and plenty of *Hallalujah, Amen, Unnnhh Hunh, That's right* from the congregation. I sat there thinking about the Flip Wilson Show, and hoping somebody would yell *watch out!,* but nobody did.

When it came time for the eulogy the place was hopping, the preacher and congregation having warmed each other up. In rhythmic cadences he called on the congregation to bless the life of Brother Dewey, their longtime friend and congregation member. *Amen! Hallelujah!*

He said that Brother Dewey was a good man, and was a credit to his community, and he had blessed the lives of all in our community. *Amen! That's right.*

He spoke of Brother Dewey's marriage to Sister Alma, also a longtime member of the congregation, and how together they had been witnesses for Christ to all they met. *Amen. Hallelujah! Unnnn Hunh!*

This went on for several minutes, a series of statements about Brother Dewey by the minister followed by calls of affirmations by the congregation. Toward the end of the eulogy when the minister started talking about Dewey going to heaven, a new voice was heard. It began very small, and grew louder and more insistent.

MINISTER: *And now we thank the Lord that Brother Dewey's earthly trials are over and he is resting, resting, resting in the bosom of Abraham.*

CONGREGATION: *Amen! Thank you Jesus!* **Well?**

MINISTER: *And even now Brother Dewey is looking down on us, and blessing us, and looking forward to the day when we will join him in his heavenly reward.* Congregation: *Amen! That's right!* **Well?**

The voice got louder and more *insistent*, and it did not have the tone of affirmation. It seemed to be saying *well I'm not too sure about that!* Somebody in the congregation thought the preacher was gilding the lily.

After the funeral, driving home, my brother and I

talked about the *well?* We were in agreement that whoever was saying *well* was insisting that Brother Dewey was *not going to heaven*. Years later I talked to a member of the congregation who had also been there. She laughed, but said I had misinterpreted the meaning of the word "well" in that context. She said that it was in fact an affirmation, something along the lines of, "Well, minister, tell us some more."

Dad laughed and marveled at what a wonderful person Alma was.

WE ARRIVED AT ST. GERTRUDE CHURCH and parked our van in the lot with cleaner, more expensive cars.

"I don't know what all these conservatives are going to think of us," Dad feigned concern as Will fetched his wheelchair from the back.

"I think we need an orthodox car," I teased, "so we don't get blacklisted again."

"It wasn't these people who blacklisted me," said Dad. "It was the worship office."

"The new pharisees," I said. "Orthodox in their anti-orthodoxy!"

Dad laughed and shushed me as Thomas wheeled him through the side door of the church.

AFTER MASS WE SAT IN THE PEWS and looked at the Emil Frei stained glass windows on the south wall—which are magnificent. To me they looked like Dad's work.

"Are you sure you didn't work on these when you worked for Emil Frei?" I asked Dad.

Dad replied that he did not and he did not want to take credit for somebody else's work. He sat and recalled names of people who may have worked with Emil Frei on the windows: Robert Frei, Robert Harmon, Frank Deck.

"It sure looks like your work," I told him.

Dad said nothing.

"Maybe these windows worked on you rather than you worked on them," I said.

"That might be true," he said. "They're great windows. Emil Frei was a great artist."

SUSIE WAS JUST GETTING HOME FROM ST. VERONICA when we pulled in the driveway.

"Any inexpressible groanings at St. Veronica?" Dad asked her at breakfast.

"No, just incomprehensible mumbling," she replied.

"No groanings at my mass either," said Dad. "I don't think the *Crisis* gang is into groaning."

AT 2:30 SUSIE TOOK WILL AND TOM SWIMMING, and Dad and I took Charlie to his basketball game. I parked Dad's wheelchair next to the scorer's table and ran the scoreboard. Charlie's basketball games were good outings for Dad, because he was indoors and close to the action. He liked football too, but often got cold. We both loved watching Charlie play, and it was a good chance for Dad to get out and about.

Charlie's friend Colin, whose family had moved to Turkey a year earlier, was in town for the summer and playing on Charlie's team. Colin's Dad worked in the US Embassy in Ankara. After the game I spoke with him about the possibility of Charlie visiting Colin in Turkey. I thought it would be a wonderful experience for Charlie. But it seemed impossible under the circumstances. Charlie was only thirteen, so either Susie or I would have to go with him, which would be expensive and logistically difficult. Susie and I were stretched with work and family commitments.

"There are direct flights from New York to Istanbul," said Collin's dad. "If you put Charlie on the plane in New York I'll take him off in Istanbul."

A light bulb went on. Later that night Charlie and I went online and looked at flights. Cost was $1,700 to $2,000 round trip which seemed expensive. Also, it did not include the cost of getting Charlie to New York and other trip expenses. But it had us thinking!

DRIVING HOME FROM BASKETBALL we stopped at Sycamore High School to pick up son Tom, who was taking down the set after the summer production of the musical *Les Miserables*. I wheeled Dad inside and talked briefly with the director. He spoke well of Tom, and hoped he would audition for future shows. We picked up pizza and some of Tom's friends came over to the house. We ate on the porch, then the young people went in the living room to watch a movie.

It was a beautiful summer evening. As darkness fell and the air cooled, Dad and I stayed on the porch, drank Jim Beam, read the paper and talked. We made a call to my sister Mary in Atlanta, and I ended up having a good talk with her husband, Jim.

Then I called my sister Ruth in Michigan, and Dad had great conversation with her. I went inside to help Susie with the dishes while Dad was on the phone. We rejoined Dad on the porch several minutes later, as he finished up his call.

"I WAS TALKING WITH AUGUSTINE," Dad

announced, when Susie, Will, and I rejoined him on the porch a while later. "He's an amazing kid." Augustine is my sister Ruth's oldest son, and Ruth had put him on the phone with Dad. He has *spina bifida*, a cross he carries with amazing grace. He is very agile and active on his braces and crutches.

"Augustine told me I'm his best friend," Dad said. "Guess what he said when I asked him why?"

We didn't know.

"Because we both have problems," said Dad.

The ceiling fan whirred. Dark shapes with low voices passed on the sidewalk outside.

"Chokes me up," said Susie.

"What a kid," said Will.

"What a family!" said Dad.

Conversation lagged, and I got more whiskey for Dad and me.

I asked Dad did he remember the time *his sister Ruth* came to visit us on the farm?

"Remind me of it," he said.

SO I TOLD HIM THE STORY. Dad's eldest sister Ruth was a Sacred Heart nun and high school math teacher. We children had only met her a couple times, and only at her convent. Her order had been cloistered and quite strict. But this was the 1960's, and the times, as Bob told us, were a changin'. Sister Ruth was permitted to visit us at home. She wore a full habit, and carried herself with much dignity and propriety.

"She was very civilized," Dad said.

She made only one visit to our little farm in Pickleville. It was memorable for us kids. I would have to think it was memorable for her also.

"It was complete culture shock for her, coming to our farm after living in a convent," Dad said.

Culture shock indeed. Flies and manure. Snot-nosed kids racing about. Chickens, cats, and dogs everywhere. Roosters crowing, cows mooing, dogs barking, kids yelling, and somebody banging out chopsticks on an old piano. Snakes, frogs, toads, lizards. Hillbillies a stone's throw away! Quite a change after convent living.

Us kids, there were probably eight or nine of us at that point, were in high-level,company-coming mode. We dressed up and Mom prepared a beautiful meal. Pegboard assignments were double-checked.

Aunt Ruth arrived and we all greeted her. She glided about the farm with Dad and Mom looking at things. We kids watched with curiosity at a respectful distance. She seemed nervous. She and Dad went in the shop, which was located in the barn, and he showed her his current projects.

Before dinner Dad went to milk the cow and Aunt Ruth sat primly on a stool in the kitchen and talked to Mom as she cooked. Mom was fantastic at making somebody feel at home and completely charmed Aunt Ruth. She was starting to look a little less stressed when Dad walked into the kitchen with a half pail of frothy fresh milk and poured it through the strainer only a few feet away from her. Then he poured it from the strainer into two-gallon jars and placed them in the refrigerator. Aunt Ruth looked grim.

We had a fine dinner, but I noticed she did not drink her milk. Dad asked her about her work and she talked about a math curriculum she was developing. She asked my older sisters about their studies and seemed pleased by my sister Anna's interest in French. She was just starting to relax again when our German Shepherd *Dakia*, who was lying under the dinner table, rubbed against her leg. She turned white and pulled her chair back from the table. We quickly removed the dog and apologized.

Somehow in the jumble she got the idea that the dog's name was *Coyote* instead of *Dakia*. For many years after that when she talked to Dad on the phone, or sent the family letter she always inquired how

Coyote was doing.

"She thought we had a damned coyote living in our house," I said.

Dad laughed and laughed and then went on to say how much he loved and missed his sister Ruth.

"It's been an enjoyable day and I'm heading for the roost pole," he said.

I held the screen door for him as he rode his scooter to his room. I got his night meds while Susie got his glass of wine. Tom was still watching the movie with his friends. Will and Charlie joined Susie and I in Dad's room for a quick night prayer.

Visit we beseech thee O Lord this house and its family
And drive far from it all snares of the enemy
Let thy holy angels dwell herein who may keep us in peace
And may your blessing be always upon us
Through our Lord Jesus Christ your son
Who lives with us now and forever
World without end, Amen.

Night fell and we slept well.

13. Abstract Prayer

Rejoice always. Pray without ceasing.
In all circumstances give thanks, for this is the will of God
for you in Christ Jesus.

1 Thessalonians 5: 16-18

Will and Charlie had already left for school. Tom was taking a shower. Dad and I sat in the dining room, talked, and drank coffee. Susie was fixing lunches and getting ready for her day teaching.

"Tom, you are using too much hot water," Susie called up the stairs. Tom liked to take *long* morning showers.

"How often does he take a shower?" Dad asked.

"Once a day," I replied.

"That's too much," Dad proclaimed.

Susie smiled at me and rolled her eyes. We had been trying to get Dad to shower twice rather than once a week.

"Have you ever smelled that boy?" I asked Dad.

"I don't think my smeller is as good as it used to be," Dad said. Thank goodness.

"Should we do the scripture reading?" I asked.

"Ready when you are," said Dad.

I wanted to try something a little different.

"Dad, I've got a reflection on prayer I'd like to do in place of the second reading," I said.

"Couldn't we do them both?" Dad said. I ignored this. We still had to do breakfast, morning medications, and clean his room, and several more things before I could move on to *my stuff*. I wanted to keep things moving!

Susie did the first reading and psalm and then I read the reflection on prayer.

It was from the Benedictine website (www.osb.org) by my former teacher Fr. Don Talafous, OSB at Saint John's University in Minnesota. He began with a reading from Matthew:

This is <u>how</u> you are to pray:

Our Father in heaven, hallowed be your name. Your kingdom come, your will be done, on earth as in heaven. Give us today our daily bread; and forgive us our debts, as we forgive our debtors; and do not subject us to the final test, but deliver us from the evil one.

Matthew 6: 9-13

Father Don focused on the use of the word *how,* rather than *what,* at the beginning of the passage. It suggests that the *Our Father* was not intended as words for repetition, but as something else. He then refers us back to a passage a little earlier in Matthew:

When praying, do not babble like the pagans, who think that they will be heard because of their many words.

Matthew 6:7

This verse is well known. What is less known or perhaps under emphasized is that it is right before the Our Father, so close that it might be considered the preamble.

"Interesting," said Dad. "The Our Father tells us how to pray, not what to say. How do we square this with the idea of praying always?"

"That's exactly what it's about," said Susie. "The Our Father tells us how to have a spirit of gratitude, peace, forgiveness, and charity all the time—in work, play, driving kids around, whatever. To me it's the opposite of the psychotic, unintelligible, repetitive, nervous mumbo jumbo we Catholics are so famous for. It's more abstract." Former May crowning queen Susie Reindl had got her fill of the Rosary growing up and had had enough!

"Amazing," said Dad. "It describes the spirit of prayer in all things. Let's say the Our Father together."

"Okay," I said. "Just once."

"We're not going to repeat it," said Susie, just loud enough that I could hear but Dad could not.

We said the Our Father *really slow*.

"JOE, COULD YOU LOOK OUTSIDE and see if there is a delivery from Suder's Art Supply?" Dad asked without looking up when I entered his room. Yellow paint splotched his hands, table, and black shirt. There was some on the canvas too. It was one of the more figurative paintings he had done in a while. I could make out a group of human figures in red and yellow, maybe a family. Dad was excited about his upcoming exhibit, and was cranking out new paintings like a machine.

"Nothing out there yet," I told Dad after checking. "How many canvases do you have left?"

"I'm on my last one," Dad said, sounding worried.

"I'll look again after lunch," I said, wanting to avoid making a run to pick up canvases if possible.

"Are you going near Kinko's today?" Dad asked. "I need a couple sketches enlarged."

"Sure," I said. He picked up a manila folder marked "sketches" beside his work table and showed me two drawings on 8½ x 11" graph paper.

"I need these blown up to 22 x 28," he said. One of the sketches caught my eye. It was a simple layout of concentric rectangles. It seemed fresh and unique.

"Do you have a name for this one?" I asked.

"I think I'll call it *Amen*," he said. "But I won't decide for sure until the painting is done."

MY BROTHER BENEDICT set another painting on the easel and then stood back to eyeball it. I adjusted the camera angle on the tripod and photographed the painting at four different settings.

"Next," I said, indicating that Ben should remove the painting and put the next one up.

"I really like this one," said Ben, not moving. We were photographing a group of Dad's new paintings at the William Schickel Gallery. We also needed to select one for the invitation to his upcoming exhibit, which would be called *Abstract Prayer*.

Ben is a talented artist with an excellent sense of color, and we sell his paintings at the gallery. He has a discriminating eye and strong views about art. He knows what he thinks and he tells me. This is sometimes helpful to an occasionally visually tone deaf person like myself trying to run an art gallery. Dad often sought Ben's opinion several times as he progressed on a painting or project.

It has perhaps been key to my relationship with Dad over many years that I am a non-artist. I have never aspired to the role of being a visual artist. I love art. I find it hugely interesting and have a decent eye. I enjoy playing the support role: managing projects, doing photography, writing, painting (walls and ceilings), and other grunt work—of which there is more than most would probably imagine. I am discovering as I write this book that it is really fun to poke fun at artists who have been making fun of me for years!

"I really like it," Ben repeated, not moving. We looked together at the painting still on the easel. It was one of several based on the sketch of concentric rectangles that had caught my eye earlier.

I turned down the radio so I could see better.

"The colors are almost tropical," Ben said. He walked to the easel, picked up the painting, and looked at the back. "It's signed, dated, and named on the back," he said. He put the painting back on the easel, and stood back to look at it again. "That's an amazing color combination."

"I don't think Dad has ever used it before," I said. But he had, I later realized. It was a combination of blacks, blues, reds, and yellows. It was very related to the color combination he used in his *Spirit* stained glass window and *Burning Bush* painting. And yet it seemed utterly unique.

"It's a smash," Ben said. "I think we should use it for the invitation."

"You're reading my mind," I said, though it may have been the other way around.

"Let's mix in a few of his older paintings with the new ones," Ben suggested. "Let's find some that people haven't seen in a while.

That seemed like a good idea too.

IT WAS A SUNNY SUNDAY AFTERNOON in downtown Loveland and the bike trail, which runs by the William Schickel Gallery, was busy. The opening reception for Dad's exhibit *Abstract Prayer*, which included a good number of his recent paintings, and a few old paintings that people hadn't seen in a while, ran from 2-4 p.m. Dad looked dapper in all black—his usual garb minus the globs of paint. He looked more domesticated than usual. My sister Joy had neatly trimmed and brushed his beard, mane, and tail.

Susie, Charlie, and I hosted, along with my sisters Joy and Lebe, and my brother Ben. Tom played the piano. Will rolled Dad's wheelchair around the gallery, and then parked him at the table where he drank red wine from a clear plastic cup and had face-to-face conversations with visitors. Several people asked him to sign the book *What a Woman! Mary Frei Schickel,* which he had completed a few months earlier. Will held books and guided his Grandpa's magic marker to a good signing spot.

"Mr. Schickel, I just love your paintings," cooed Cindy from Cindy's Friendly Tavern as she put her arm around him and got right in his face. The wattage of Dad's bulb went up considerably, as Cindy and two other women from the bar made a big fuss over him.

The opening went well. There was a good turnout: friends, family, invitees, bikers in spandex, clergy in mufti, and art interlopers in corduroy. Dad saw a good number of people he had not seen in a while.

"THAT WAS A VERY NICE EVENT," Dad declared as we drove home from the opening. "Did we sell any paintings?"

"Two," I said.

"Not bad," he said.

"We've done worse," I said. "Your recent paintings are very reasonably priced."

"True," he said. His seat belt alarm went off.

"Just ignore it," I said. "We're almost home."

"Is the Cadillac Rule still in effect?" he asked as I rolled his wheelchair up the ramp. Over the years he and I had *many* discussions about who does and does not buy art, particularly *his* art. We had come to the conclusion that people in foreign cars and old cars were our better market. A Cadillac driver was not a good prospect.

"I'm not sure," I said. "Loveland is getting busier and people park all over the place. I don't see their cars like I used to."

Dad cogitated on this for a moment.

"You're just a bigot!" I told him as I steadied his transfer from wheelchair to rocking chair. "Give those poor Cadillac owners a chance!"

"I have to be prejudiced against *somebody!*" he protested. He paused for a moment then rambled on.

"I'm glad the group from Cindy's Tavern showed up."
He paused again. "I'm not prejudiced against Harley
owners. There are lots of Harleys at Cindy's."

"Did a Harley owner ever buy a painting from
you?" I asked.

"Yes," he replied.

"Who?"

"Dave Dickstein."

"That was when I was about five years old," I
protested.

"Doesn't matter," he said looking smug. "Now
would you be so kind as to get me a little whiskey?"

"Sure Dad." I went to get it.

"Mr. Marketing Genius!" he yelled after me.

Joseph Schickel

14. Family Reunion

Then Abraham gave up the ghost, and died in a good old age, an old man, and full of years; and was gathered to his people. And his sons Isaac and Ishmael buried him in the cave of Machpelah, in the field of Ephron the son of Zohar the Hittite, which is before Mamre; The field which Abraham purchased of the sons of Heth: there was Abraham buried, and Sarah his wife.

Genesis 25: 8-10

My Ford Taurus flew along the New York Thruway in Upstate New York near Syracuse. Dad rode shotgun wearing his Notre Dame Cap. My sister,

Lebe, rode in back. We were headed for the family reunion in Geneva, New York. My goal was to make it there with the fewest possible bathroom breaks.

"How many are coming to the reunion?" Dad asked.

"Pretty many," Lebe said. "I heard it was over 180."

"We're a big family," Dad said smugly. He *obviously* took pride in his prolific progeny.

Silence. What could one say? As a topic for family conversation it was *the* living dead horse—kicked around, knocked up, and played out.

"Dad, I think it's really cool that your brothers will be there," Lebe said, steering the discussion toward something that could be coherently discussed. Dad's four living brothers; Hubert, Gerald, Jack, and Lou were all planning to attend.

The extended Schickel family is large, loud, and opinionated. In two generations we went from staunch German Catholic to mini United Nations. White, brown, black, and yellow. Catholic, Protestant, Muslim, atheist, agnostic. Gay, straight, lesbian. Stick shift or automatic. Engineer, lawyer, artist, politician, builder, musician. Rag-head, bald, Afro, Vaseline, and Dapper Dan. Push start or pull start. Republican, Democrat, Nazi, Communist, and Jew. *Many* are loud and opinionated. And many have the "Schickel gene"—which the rest of the world might describe as *excessive moralistic self-righteousness*. Somewhere in the German Catholic ghetto a Puritan stud got over the wall. Lotsa open pie holes and finger wagging at a Schickel family reunion.

"I hope this isn't too hard on Susie," Dad said, "you being gone for four days."

"It's fine," I said, looking over my shoulder at my sister Lebe riding in back, who shook her head and laughed quietly.

She knew, as I did, that Susie and the boys were *thrilled* to have me and Dad out of the house for four days. They would get along just fine. They would kick back, relax, chill, watch movies, stay up late, eat popcorn, and sleep in in the morning. All the things that were difficult when Dad was around, and almost impossible when Dad and Grandpa were both around.

SHOULD WE LISTEN TO SOME MUSIC?" I asked, wanting to show off my first iPod.

"Sure," said Dad.

I found *Midnight Train to Georgia* by Gladys Knight and the Pips, a song I knew Dad loved, and cranked it up. Gladys wailed, the Pips (her amazing male backup singers) sailed, Dad made kung fu motions in the air. The old Taurus edged up over 90 mph before I reined her in slightly. Lebe sang with Gladys and I did backup do-wops with the Pips. We were haulin' ass!

He's leavin', on a midnight train to Georgia,
I'd rather live in his world,
than live without him in mine.

"What a great song," Dad said. "Just beautiful."

We listened to Bob Dylan, Gordon Lightfoot, Joan Baez, Over The Rhine, and Cat Stevens, and a couple of original songs by my son, the great singer/songwriter Tom Schickel.

SCRUB PINES CLUNG TO CRAGGY ROCKS around the Finger Lakes.

"What do you call land that is too rocky to actually grow anything?" asked Dad, peering out at the rough country.

Silence. Lebe and I don't know.

"Dairy country," said Dad.

"Who told you that?" Lebe asked.

"Norbert," Dad said. Dad's older brother, soulmate, and confidante Norbert, had been a dairy farmer in these parts. Among other things.

Dad and Norbert. Brothers and best friends. What a pair! Like two ass cheeks. Chips off the same flinty block. Notre Dame grads. Navy pilot turned real estate developer. Boxer turned artist. Implacable, self-righteous, and apparently charming Catholic vagabonds who married well, and brought their well healed and surely shell shocked brides to ramshackle farms where they increased, multiplied, and poured their considerable energy and meager resources into a thousand projects that didn't make much money. They talked on the phone several times a week. Making the next mortgage payment was usually one of the subjects of the call.

"It's like they were trying to do a Catholic Worker version of Monticello," said my cousin Sarto Schickel years later.

"Norbert was my Theo," said Dad, referring to Vincent Van Gogh's brother and supporter, Theo. "He believed in me as an artist. He always supported me. I was so lucky to have a brother like that. I don't know how I would have survived without him. I would have been a very different person."

WE GATHERED UNDER A BIG WHITE TENT at a little resort called Geneva On The Lake, in

Geneva, New York. My cousin Bill Schickel, who was manager of the resort, beamed proudly as he approached the microphone and welcomed some 200 members of the extended Schickel family to the reunion.

"I can't hear," Dad said, putting his hand to his ear. I wheeled him closer to one of the speakers.

ON JULY 15, 1870 France declared war on Prussia, starting the Franco-Prussian War. On that same day two anxious German parents, Johannes and Gertruda Schickel, penned a letter to their son Wilhelm, who had just immigrated to America. Cousin Bill then proceeded to read the letter:

Wiesbaden, Germany
July 15, 1870
Dear Wilhelm,
Travel with God, then no mishap will befall thee! Hold fast to your holy religion, to which you are pledged! Be on your guard against every sin and avoid every occasion which could bring you to a fall. Let prayer be your daily weapon; never omit the practices of your holy religion. Do not forget your dear parents and think of your faithful brothers and sisters. Be for them, if you can, father and provider. Remember also your good grandparents and lock them into your daily prayer.

In your vocation may you become always more proficient, and be a man of character. Be hard-working and frugal; that will save you from want. Increase your property, but not at the expense of uprightness and loyalty. Be loving towards all, and have a heart for those who suffer want. Take care of your health; but more still think of your eternal happiness!

Let this memorandum be written in your heart. Then our reunion, be it here or there, will be a happy one.

Your parents, who will always beat you in their heart,

Johannes and Gertruda Schickel

A reflective quiet settled over us as we took a moment to let the letter sink in.

"Who can fail to be inspired by this letter?" Cousin Bill marveled.

"I love that line, *beat you in their heart*," said Dad laughing.

Wilhelm Schickel had done well, becoming a famous New York architect who did hundreds of buildings, many of which stand today and are on historic registers. There were lots of pictures of him and his buildings at the reunion. The other featured piece of family history was the Schickel Motorcycle, which was developed and manufactured by Norbert

H. Schickel, one of Wilhelm's sons and my grandfather. As this book is being written, Norbert H. Schickel is about to be inducted into the American Motorcycle Association Hall of Fame in Las Vegas, Nevada, see www.SchickelMotorcycle.com. There were books, pictures, and two actual motorcycles at the reunion.

"SO BILL WHAT ARE YOU WORKING ON THESE DAYS?" asked his brother Lou. Dad was the eldest of his five living brothers. Lou, Hubert, Jerry, and Jack, were sitting with him at a table on the beautiful terrace at Geneva On The Lake. Dad's late brother Norbert's wife, Marnie, was also there, and they were having a great time. The brothers lived at a distance (Arkansas, Arizona, Florida, New York, and Ohio) and were not really close—but stayed somewhat in touch and enjoying catching up. Being closer, and staying more in touch, clearly appealed to all of them at this point in their lives. Dad was the eldest by several years, and clearly the most frail, the only one using a wheelchair. Group conversations like this were difficult for him to follow. Seeing and hearing people who were not smack dab in his face, was difficult. But he clearly enjoyed just being with them, even if he couldn't hear all the conversation.

Dad told them about his paintings, and daily routines, and then sat back, smiled, nodded, and allowed the others to carry the conversation.

LEBE, DAD, AND I HAD A BEAUTIFUL ROOM at Geneva On The Lake.

"Bill and Lou get a lot of credit," said Dad. My cousin Bill and Uncle Lou were the driving force behind this family reunion.

"Dad, tell me about your sister Agnes," said Lebe.

"She was the pious one," said Dad. "We thought she might become a nun. Instead she became the mother of a big family. Nobody thought Ruth would become a nun. But she did. It's amazing how that stuff goes. God writes straight in crooked lines."

THE FORD TAURUS WAS HEADING HOME and I was flipping through podcasts on my iPod.

"That woman has a wonderful speaking voice," Dad said. "Can you go back to that?"

I went back. She had a *great* voice — clear, intelligent, and richly feminine—which enthralled Dad instantly. He would have been happy to listen to her reciting the phone book. But she was talking about an old man named Abraham, who at the age of 90 fathered a child named Isaac. Now Dad was really interested. He held himself a little straighter in the seat.

Her name was Krista Tippett and she was interviewing an author named Bruce Filer. Many years earlier at his Bar Mitzvah, Filer had recited the Genesis 12 passages which direct Abraham to go forth to the land which God will show him, leaving his ancestors and their idol worship behind. This Abraham does, and he becomes the original iconic monotheist, the father of the three great religions of the book: Judaism, Islam, and Christianity.

Filer was a mostly secular Jew who became a journalist and writer. After 9/11 he reflected deeply on what he saw as the defining crisis of our era—the bloody and acrimonious feud among Islam, Judaism, and Christianity. He recalled Genesis 12 from his Bar Mitzvah, and he thought it might contain a key, in the person of old father Abraham.

Abraham had two sons. Ishmael, his first born by his *servant* Haggar, is his ancestral link to Islam. Isaac, born to his *wife* Sarah, is his ancestral link to Judaism and Christianity. Abraham almost killed Isaac at God's command, but stopped at the last moment, also at God's command. Barren Sarah laughed when Abraham suggested she would have a child at age 75, but she got serious about the inheritance once Isaac was born. She demanded that Abraham banish Ishmael and his mother to the desert and almost certain death. It's a classic family conflict, with bad blood and a definite rift.

A couple of miracles later (Isaac and Ishmael both survived) and generations hence—an amazing and hopeful event occurred. When Abraham died there was a family reunion of sorts as Ishmael and Isaac come together to bury their father in present day Hebron.

The whole span of Abraham's life was one hundred and seventy-five years. Then he breathed his last, dying at a ripe old age, grown old after a full life; and he was taken to his kinsmen. His sons Isaac and Ishmael buried him in the cave of Machpelah, in the field of Ephron, son of Zohar the Hittite, which faces Mamre, the field that Abraham had bought from the Hittites; there he was buried next to his wife Sarah.

Genesis 25: 7-10

Author Bruce Filer finds hope in the little-known (or perhaps under-emphasized) biblical fact that Isaac and Ishmael, after much acrimony and separation, came together to bury their father. He thinks it's time to emphasize this story.

"That's amazing," said Dad.

"It doesn't say they sat down to dinner together," I said, "or that they agreed to meet again next year."

"But they might have done that," said Dad. "Just because it's not in scripture doesn't mean it didn't happen."

"The fact that they came together at all is inspiring," said Lebe.

CONVERSATION LAGGED and Dad snoozed. I called Susie on the cell phone, but she didn't pick up. She and the boys were probably swimming. I left a message that we would be home in the late afternoon. Her vacation was almost over.

"Joe, this has really been fun," said Lebe from the back seat. "I'm so glad we did it. It really meant a lot to all the family to have Dad there."

"I think it meant a lot to Dad too," I said.

We crossed the state line back into Ohio.

Joseph Schickel

15. Gethsemani

The quality of mercy is not strain'd,
It droppeth as the gentle rain from heaven
upon the place beneath.
It is twice blest:
It blesseth him that gives and him that takes.
William Shakespeare
Merchant of Venice, Act 4 Scene 1

FACE TO FACE

*Then Jesus went with his disciples to a place called
Gethsemane, and he said to them, "Sit here while I go over
there and pray."*
Luke 26:36-39

"Joe is going on retreat to Gethsemani," Susie
told Dad after I left. She was putting prescription
ointment on his scalp, which was tender and sensitive.
Dad was enjoying the attention.

"Retreat? Retreat from what?" Dad asked. "He's
needed here. Sounds more like surrender to me."

"He's doing a photo shoot for the book," Susie
said.

"Oh, that's right. When will he be back?"

"Tomorrow," said Susie.

"Susie, can you find my hearing aid? I think I
dropped it on the floor."

Susie's heart rate jumped. A month earlier Dad
had crushed a hearing aid under the rail of his
rocking chair. Insurance covered the replacement but
it was a pain.

"Don't move Dad," she said, dropping to her
knees and sweeping the floor around the rocker with
her hands.

"Did you find it?" Dad asked. "I really need it."

"Here it is," she said, handing it to him. Crisis averted.

"Thank God," he said, inserting it in his ear, then holding his head still and listening to see if it was working. "Great, it's working."

There was a loud crash out in the dining room, followed by an angry exchange between Tom and Will.

"Excuse me Dad," said Susie. "I have to stop a fight."

I LISTENED TO THE *NEW YORK TIMES BOOK REVIEW* PODCAST in the solitary splendor of my just cleaned Ford Taurus, and drove at a calm and legal rate of speed, down I-75 toward Louisville. It was a beautiful Sunday afternoon and I was *on retreat*! Praying. Being holy. Living on a higher plane. I called Susie on my cell phone to gloat.

"I'm on retreat, sweetheart," I said. "I've just been working so hard I need a little time off. Now don't call me unless it's *really* important."

"You are vile," Susie growled. "And your Dad agrees with me."

"No he doesn't," I said. "You're just being petty and small. Why can't you be more like me?"

"Father Joe," she muttered. "I married a damn

priest."

"Goodbye sweetheart. I have to go pray now." I resumed the podcast, smiled smugly, and exited I-75, found Hwy 247, and drove into the knobs of Kentucky.

DAD HAD A HIGH REGARD FOR THE MONASTIC WAY OF LIFE and for the monks he knew. Maybe I inherited the gene from him. I visited Gethsemani with him as a kid during the renovation project and got a taste of the Cistercian way of life. The monks at Gethsemani are Trappists, formally called the Order of Cistercians of Strict Observance, or the O.C.S.O.'s. They ran a big farm, observed the great silence, ate simple food, and prayed a lot. Gethsemani's daily schedule for the Liturgy of the Hours, originally prescribed by the Rule of St. Benedict, is below :

Vigils at 3:15am
Lauds at 5:45 am
Eucharist at 6:15 am
Terce at 7:30 am
Sext at 12:15 pm
None at 2:15 pm

Vespers at 5:30 pm
Rosary at 7:00 pm
Compline at 7:30 pm

They didn't call it strict for nothing. Their most famous resident, the monk/writer/celebrity Thomas Merton (Father Louis), put Gethsemani on the map. His well-documented antics also lent credence to O.C.S.O.'s other meaning—Often Caught Sneaking Out.

I went to college at Saint John's University in Minnesota. It is run by the Benedictines of Saint John's Abbey, which at the time was the largest Benedictine abbey in North America. The Order of St. Benedict, the O.S.B.'s, are not at all strict by comparison. They are not a contemplative order, but rather are involved in many more outward-looking endeavors, including the staffing of local parishes, and operating a high school and university which are on the same grounds. Their observance of the Liturgy of the Hours is less elaborate. The monks left the abbey grounds all the time and I never got the impression they had to sneak.

I ARRIVED AT GETHSEMANI at 5:00 p.m.,

checked in with the Guestmaster, found my room, and went to Vespers at 5:30. Brother Paul Quenon, OCSO met me after vespers and we had a bite with a couple of other late arrivals. Brother Paul, who sleeps under the stars even during winter, looked younger than his sixty-nine years. He was born in West Virginia and came to Gethsemani at eighteen after reading *Seven Story Mountain* in 1958. He said before reading Thomas Merton's famous book, he thought that to find a monastery you had to go to Europe. He's a renowned Merton scholar and a widely published and exhibited photographer. He is also monastic cultural director, and inquired whether Susie might come and do a piano accompaniment for Carlos Zavala's cello for the monks in the chapter room some time. Our friend Carlos Zavala, recently retired from the Cincinnati Symphony Orchestra, visits Gethsemani regularly. Brother Paul has fond memories of Dad, and asked to be remembered to him. He was a strong supporter of the abbey renovation project along with Merton.

Dad's design for the renovation of the Abbey Church at Gethsemani was one of the crowning jewels of his career. It was widely published and photographed and attracted lots of attention. Dad received several awards, including a Gold Medal

Award for excellence in architectural design from the American Institute of Architects. To the best of my knowledge he is one of the few non-architects to ever receive this award. Lots of people think Dad was an architect but he was not, and was careful to say and write that he was not, publicly and often.

"Dad, you are an architect in the metaphysical, historical, common meaning of the term. You are not an architect in its shallow, legalistic, paranoid, money-grubbing, self-promoting, bureaucratic, monopolistic, lying, cheating, back-stabbing, bed-wetting sense," I told him while we worked one day.

"Stop your shit stirring," he said. "We've got bills to pay, projects to complete, and mouths to feed."

"But if I don't stir it—it won't stink," I said.

"You're arguing my case very well," said Dad.

WHEN THE GETHSEMANI RENOVATION WAS COMPLETED Father Louis (Thomas Merton) sent Dad a handwritten note which read:

Dear Bill,

I just wanted to tell you what a splendid job I think you have done in our Abbey Church and the Cloister. I particularly like the interior of the church—bright, simple, clear-cut, no nonsense and perfectly in accord with the spirit of our life. Also I am glad to recognize that it is still my Abbey Church, the place of my vows and first Mass – without its ancient defects.

Fr. Louis (Thomas Merton)

GETHSEMANI. THE PEACE OF THE PLACE drenches like a gentle rain. I slept hard. At three a.m. I woke to a slow gong as a big bell tolled once. I looked at the clock, rolled over, and was going back to sleep when I heard robes rustle quietly past my door. Remembering that Vigils was at 3:15, I dressed quickly, went to the chapel, and sat in the balcony. Vigils had already begun. The monks were sitting in the dark chanting, using only small reading lights when necessary. It was hauntingly beautiful.

I BEGAN MY PHOTO SHOOT at 8:00 a.m.

"It's a light show that changes every minute" said Brother Paul, as we discussed photographing the interior of the Abbey Church. "You have to move fast."

How right he was. Blue, grey, brown, and yellow refracted morning light from the immense stained glass windows of the east wall of the nave undulated, mixed, separated, and remixed as it quickly moved down and across the sheer vertical white of the west wall. I was a highly un-monastic whirling dervish as I raced to get my shots; sweating, muttering, shutter clicking, tripod clattering. As first I shot only when the church was empty, dashing in between prayer times, but Brother Paul encouraged me to be bolder, and shoot the monks as they entered, prayed, sang, bowed, knelt, and exited.

"This is not a museum," he said firmly. "We are a living, breathing human community."

The challenge, I discovered was to get both the *light show*, and the sense of an *abbey church*, together, at the same time, in the same photograph if possible. It was like pulling together two polar opposites—the dramatic, organic *light show*—and the dignified, serene *abbey church*. I worked my tail off for about five hours, and got some pretty good shots.

I WAS SHOOTING PHOTOS OF THE CLOISTERWALK. Sun drenched the polished pebbles in the exposed aggregate floor of the long hall. I had the shot all set up when the heavy wood door at the far end of the hallway opened slowly, and a robed monk riding a scooter appeared. He smiled broadly as he approached. His right hand navigated the controls and left hand held a coffee mug. It was Father Matthew Kelty, OSCO, Dad's longtime friend. He rolled to a stop.

"Did your Dad get his scooter?" he asked.

"Yes he did, and it's working great," I said.

"I'm glad to hear it," said Fr. Matthew. "I love mine. Greet him for me."

"I will do that," I said. "He sends greeting to you."

"He's a great guy," said Matthew. "I wish he would come and visit me."

"Maybe next year," I said. "He's a bit under the weather."

"I'm sorry to hear that," he said as the scooter rolled away. He was making the rounds, and had places to go. "I will keep him in my prayers….," he called as the scooter rounded the corner and went out of sight

Joseph Schickel

.

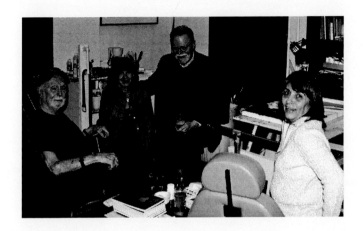

16. Lion in the Winter

The Lion was cold! A harsh winter, poor mobility, and a drafty old house conspired against him. We kept his room at 83 degrees and brought him hot coffee, foot rubs, hot water bottles, heat blanket bottles, whiskey, vodka, and wine. I put a huge thermometer on the wall of his room. He looked skeptical when I told him the room temperature.

He huddled under blankets and shivered. Making the rounds and outdoor walks stopped. A couple of times the pilot light on his gas fireplace in his room went out. We scrambled to get electric heaters going while Thomas tinkered with the stove and got it going.

Filling his day with meaningful activity became a big challenge.

"I can't walk, or see, or hear very well. But there are still twenty four hours in a day," he told me one day.

IT WAS A COLD, SUNNY MORNING IN FEBRUARY, and time for Dad's ten o'clock walk.

"Good morning, Pop," I said, walking into his room.   Dad was sitting in his rocking chair, looking blue.

"Good morning, Joe," he said. "Could you check that thermostat? I'm feeling cold." The wall thermometer said 83 degrees.

"I'll turn it up a little," I said, nudging it up a few degrees and then removing my sweater. Old age has a lot of Catch 22's. When you're lonely you get cold easily. But if you keep the room really warm, it's hard for people to visit with you for very long. I'm a headlong person with a fast metabolism. I broke a sweat almost immediately when I sat down in Dad's room. We sat together and talked about the day.

"Is there anything coming at me today?" Dad asked.

"John is coming to visit you this afternoon," I

said. "I thought you two might do the afternoon rounds together."

"That sounds good," Dad said. "I'm afraid it will be too cold for me to make the rounds by myself.

"Should we do your morning walk?" I asked.

"I would like that," Dad said. "How is the heat in the living room."

"I've got the gas stove going and the pocket doors closed," I said. "It should be nice and warm."

Dad looked like he didn't believe me. Dad's room and the living room have gas fireplaces and can be kept toasty and warm—so Dad spends a good amount of his time in these rooms. The living room is also nice and sunny, which he likes occasionally. Bright sun bothers his eyes after a short time.

"Are you sure the living room fireplace is on?" Dad asked.

"I turned it on and closed the pocket doors about ten minutes ago," I said. "Are you ready for your warm-up?"

"Ready," he said. "Is the path clear?" Once Dad was on his feet he needed an unobstructed path through the front room to his couch in the living room.

"The path is clear," I said. "I've got the piano bench pulled out in case you want to stop and rest halfway."

"Stay close in case I need help," he said, and off we went.

I grabbed his belt in back and helped him to his feet, then held on as he made his way, with difficulty, out of his room, through the front room, past the piano bench, into the living room, and over to the couch.

"Whew, barely made it," he said, landing heavily on the corner of the couch.

"Good job," I said. "You should probably rest a bit before your long run. I've got something I want to read to you."

"What is that?" he asked.

"It's a Lenten reflection by Fr. Don Talafous, OSB, one of my old teachers at Saint John's University in Minnesota," I said.

"I would like to hear it," he said.

And so I read it to him. "If you wish to be my disciple," Jesus says "you must take up <u>your</u> cross each day, and follow in my steps." (Luke 9:23). According to Fr. Don the word "your" merits reflection. *Our crosses are there and we know what they are.* It isn't like we have to go looking for something to give up like candy, or whiskey. Fr. Talafous quotes François Mauriac who says the only true crosses are the ones we do not choose. A difficult person to work with, a nagging physical problem, compulsive or addictive behavior of any kind. The crosses we choose, and then talk about, are as meaningless and cheap as Hollywood bling-bling.

"Amazing," Dad said. "That's just excellent. It's not hard to figure out what my crosses are."

"Or mine," I said. "Are you ready for your long run?" I asked.

"You mean my long *ride*." Dad said.

I moved the stationary bike over next to the couch, and then helped him get up on it. He was weak, and it took a good heave on his belt to get him up there.

"Five minutes," he said. "Time me."

At this point Dad wanted me to stand there and watch the clock while he rode, hopefully for five minutes. Perhaps unbeknownst to him, I had a few things I needed to get done. So as often as not I tried to duck out for a few minutes while he rode, and then come back in three or four minutes. I tried to do this today, but he must have sensed that I was going.

"How long is it now?" he asked pointedly.

"Two minutes," I said, guessing. "Three minutes to go." I stayed.

"Five minutes," I said, when his time was up. I

helped him off the stationary bike and back to the couch. "That was pretty good," I told him. "Should we read a little *Cold Sassy*?

"Sure, if you have time," he said. "I wonder how old Rucker and Miss Love Simpson are getting along?"

The book *Cold Sassy Tree* by Olive Ann Burns was a warm comfort in that cold winter. It's about a young boy named Will Tweedy coming of age in the little town of Cold Sassy, Georgia in the early 1900's. Dad loved the rural humor and strongly identified with Will's grandfather, the old codger Rucker Blakeslee who owned the general store. Rucker scandalized the town by marrying a *much younger woman*, Miss Love Simpson, *too soon* after his wife passed away. "It's kind of embarrassing," my sister Lebe had said, commenting on Dad's fascination with the couple.

"Remind me what was going on." Dad said.

I reviewed the story with Dad. Old Rucker and Miss Love had caused such a scandal that they no longer felt welcome at their regular church in Cold Sassy. So they had their own service at home.

"So there was a *Church of What's Hap'nin' Now* in Cold Sassy too," said Dad.

"I guess there was," I said. I reminded Dad that when we last read, old Rucker was telling his grandson, Will, about the home church service he and Miss Love had.

Rucker was the preacher and Miss Love was the *pi-anna* player. And it turned out old Rucker liked to preach, and the fact that there was only one person in the congregation, his wife, didn't slow him down. When Miss Love got tired of it and tried to cut him off, Rucker took offense, and asked her if Methodists interrupt and argue with the preacher or listen to what he's got to say?

Dad laughed. "Those two are great," he said.

"Miss Love was a handful," I said.

"Rucker—was the handful," called Susie from the next room.

No response from Dad or me. Dad probably didn't hear her.

"Why do you think she married old Rucker?" Dad asked.

"For a variety of reasons," I offered. Dad looked at me quizzically and sat thinking for a moment.

"*Because he asked her*," Dad said with finality.

He sat there shaking his head slightly and thinking. He thought asking Mom to marry him was the brashest move he ever made as a young man. And he marveled the rest of his life that she said yes and her parents supported the idea.

"Should we read a little more?" I asked.

"Only if you have time, Joe. You know I love it."

WE READ ON. Old Rucker was still playing preacher, and now he told young Will that he didn't care whether Jesus rose from the dead. It just wasn't important, he explained. What was important was the way he inspired the disciples. "They quit settin round a-moanin' and a-tremblin', and got to work," Rucker said. That's what was important.

"It's an interesting comment but old Rucker was wrong," said Dad.

"What do you mean?" I asked, but I knew where he was going. Dad was pretty orthodox in his religious beliefs.

"It's important that Jesus rose from the dead," Dad declared.

I knew he was about to quote Flannery O'Conner so I beat him to the punch.

"It's all bullshit if it's just a story," I said. "If it didn't actually happen I'm not interested. Dad, old Rucker wasn't much of a theologian was he?"

"No, but Jesus wasn't either, and I like both of them," said Dad.

"How can you like Rucker? He's a damn heretic,"

I said, baiting the lion.

"I'm not saying I agree with him, I just like him," said Dad laughing. "I don't always agree with you either. But I try my damnedest to like you. You might give me a little more help! You might go get us a snort of Jim Beam!"

"Too early for me," I said. Drinking Jim Beam before noon was not a good idea for either of us. "But you go ahead."

"You're right," he said. "I better get back to my room. I'm feeling a bit weak today so I think I'll skip the third leg of my run. Could you bring the scooter in here and I'll ride it back."

I went in his room, sat in his scooter, and rode it into the living room. I helped him aboard, then joined him in his room a minute later, and helped him transfer from the scooter to his rocking chair.

"Who's here for lunch?" Dad asked as I left.

"Susie, you, and I," I said. "I'll have your glass of wine out at 11:45."

"Thanks, Joe," Dad said. "That's a great book."

KENTUCKY STATE SENATOR JOHN SCHICKEL, showed up at 2:00 to make the rounds with Dad. Dad was really looking forward to it. John parked his Toyota 4Runner outside Dad's door with the heater running, then came in to get Dad. Dad was sitting in his rocker with his coat and hat on, ready to go. John helped him from his rocker into his wheelchair. Out the door and down the ramp they went. Yes!

Having a sibling with Dad for several hours was the very definition of freedom for Susie and me that winter. When family members asked me what they could do to help, I always said the same thing. Spend more time face to face or on the phone with Dad.

Dad's vision and hearing were bad and getting worse. Human conversation was the warm mothers milk he craved at all times but more than ever that cold winter. Dinner conversation was becoming inaccessible; he simply could not hear most of it. Raising my voice beyond a certain level at the dinner table, so he could hear, seemed out of place. It was getting where conversation had to be one-on-one, face-to-face, and loud.

Or on the phone! Phone conversation with Dad was easier than face-to-face in some ways. The volume on his receiver was turned up so he could hear. He could not dial very well despite the oversized buttons. The boys, Susie, and I often dialed numbers for him when he wanted to call someone.

"He doesn't have any trouble dialing my number,"

said Susie.

"HOW WAS YOUR OUTING?" I asked.

Dad and John were back in his room, talking and having a great time. They were drinking whiskey, laughing, and John was stinking up the house with a cigar.

"Just great!" Dad said. "We drove down by the old farm."

"We walked around up at Costco too," said John.

"Dad, did John tell you he might stay here when we take our trip in late March?" I asked.

"Yes he did," Dad said. "It sounds like a great plan."

"I'm pretty excited about it," I said.

THOUGH WE HAD NOT YET PURCHASED THE AIRLINE TICKET, it looked like the plans for Charlie to go to Turkey were coming together. He would spend ten days there with his friend Colin's family. Susie and I would put him on a direct flight at Kennedy Airport and Colin's parents would take him off in Istanbul. Susie, Will, Tom and I would drop Charlie off at the Kennedy Airport, and then spend a few days in New York. John would stay with Dad while we were gone.

"How was your trip to Gethsemani?" John asked. I had spent a couple days at the Abbey of Gethsemani in Kentucky earlier in the week shooting photos for the new book on Dad's work.

"It went fine," I said. "It's a wonderful place."

"Joe saw my old friend Matthew Kelty," said Dad. "He has a scooter just like mine." Father Matthew Kelty, OSCO had been good friends with Dad since the 1960's, when Dad designed the renovation of the abbey church. The famous writer and monk Thomas Merton (Father Louis) had been on the building committee and the project got a lot of attention. About six months earlier, when Dad had been struggling with the decision about whether to get a scooter, he had talked with Matthew Kelty on the telephone. The fact that Matthew Kelty had a scooter, and loved it, made it more palatable to Dad. He got one and it was a huge help.

THE FRONT DOOR SLAMMED, a book pack clunked heavily on the front room floor, and my son Charlie stuck his head into Grandpa's room.

"Hi Grandpa, hi Uncle John," said Charlie, wearing his grey St. Columban hooded sweatshirt. "Dad, can I play outside with Amons?"

"Hi Charlie," we said together. He tried to make a

quick escape but I caught him.

"Charlie, tell Grandpa and Uncle John about your trip to Turkey," I said.

"Oh, yeah, well ….. I might be going to Turkey in March.   Can I go play with Amons *right now* Dad?" said Charlie, who *loved* to play outside with our neighbors after school. His eyes pleaded for release from captivity.

"Your trip sounds wonderful, Charlie," said Dad.

"What a great opportunity," said John.

"Change out of your school uniform and get a snack before you go play," I said.

Charlie fled the room. His feet pounded the stairs like a drum roll as he raced to his room to change. It took him maybe sixty seconds to change, descend the stairs with a crash, and grab a snack. The door slammed again and I saw him racing across the yard. Freedom!

WE WERE SHIFTING INTO AFTER SCHOOL MODE. Susie had students at Loveland Music Center until 6:30. Charlie played outside, Tom pounded his keyboard above us, Will lifted weights after school. Dad started painting and I started getting supper.   At 4:00 we would do another indoor walk and read more *Cold Sassy*. At 5:00 I would bring him a whiskey.

John and I talked in the kitchen before he left.

"How do you think Dad is doing?" I asked.

"His mobility is down and he seems really frail," said John. "I don't think the rest of the family realizes what he's like."

"Susie and I have talked about that," I said. "The Loveland siblings see him a lot so they know. Others have a mental picture of him from six months or a year ago and it's changed a lot. Did Susie tell you what Amy Dickinson said?"

"No," said John. His attention perked up when I mentioned the famous advice columnist, who recently married one of our many cousins. "Tell me."

"She said that many people of Dad's generation have never spent a lot of time on their own, and it's difficult for them. Our generation had smaller families and married later so we got used to having time alone."

"I believe it," said John. "Dad wants somebody with him all the time."

"I did not anticipate how much he would crave companionship," I said.

"You and Susie are doing a great job," said John. "Are you getting the help you need?"

"Yes and no," I said. "The more visitors the better. Phone calls are great too. Days when he doesn't have visitors get really long. Ben calls and visits him every day which is a huge help."

"I wish I could come more often," John said. "It's hard with traffic and work. I'll try to call more."

"I can't tell you how much I appreciate your offer to stay here during our trip," I said.

John climbed into his 4Runner and fled for Kentucky.

AFTER SUPPER DAD AND I MADE THE ROUNDS TOGETHER, dropping off and picking up—Charlie to basketball; Tom to play rehearsal; Dad, Ben, and I to Starbucks.

Later Dad and I sat together in his room and read more *Cold Sassy*. Rucker, Miss Love and young Will were talkin' bout religion, and holy stuff, and Dad really enjoyed it.

Will Tweedy asked his Grandpa did he think Grandma was in heaven? Rucker responded that if there was a heaven, Grandma was surely there. When Will asked if he believed in heaven he responded that unfortunately there was only one way to know for sure.

"And I'm not thet curious," Rucker said.

"He's amazing," Dad said. "In some ways he reminds me of me. In other ways he's completely different." I didn't want him to elaborate, so I read on. Young Will and his Grandpa were still talking about religion. Will was skeptical about the power of prayer, and told his Grandpa that he had prayed fervently and often for a million dollars, but never got at dime.

"Thet was just wishin'. Hit warn't prayn'," said Rucker.

I WENT TO GET DAD'S NIGHT MEDS and Susie brought his glass of wine. He was still laughing when I returned.

"I love that book, Joe," Dad said. "It's been a great companion these last few weeks."

Susie, Tom, and I gathered for night prayer.

Visit we beseech the oh Lord
this house and its family,
And drive far from it all snares of the enemy
Let thy hold angels dwell herein
who may keep us on peace
And let thy blessing be always upon us....

Good nights. Sleep wells. Hugs. A half hour later his light went off.

Joseph Schickel

17. Turkey & New York

Where are you?" Dad asked.

"Leaving Manhattan and heading for Kennedy Airport," I replied. "We're about to go through the tunnel into Queens. I better hang up and focus on driving."

"I'm doing fine," Dad said. "John is taking good care of me. Tell Charlie to have a great trip."

"Thanks Pop," I said. "We'll talk soon."

IT WAS RAINY AND GREY AT KENNEDY AIRPORT. We parked the van and approached the cavernous international terminal.

"They said one of us could take Charlie right up to his gate, right?" said Susie. Her thirteen-year old son was about to fly halfway around the world, alone. It was kinda scary.

"Absolutely," I said. I had called Turkish Airlines when I booked his flight and they assured me that since Charlie was a minor—either Susie or I would be able to accompany him to the gate for departure.

"IT'S A SECURITY RULE. Only ticketed passengers can go to the gate." said the tired looking Turk at the Turkish Airlines counter. "Your son will be fine." His thick accent was not reassuring. He had just told us that thirteen-year-old Charlie would have to clear security, find his departure gate, and board the plane —by himself—on the main concourse of JFK's international terminal. From where we stood at security clearance, Charlie's gate was nowhere to be seen—only dozens of signs for hundreds of gates— probably miles and bus or tram rides away. The terminal was huge and the faces mostly brown. There was the din of many languages that were not English.

"That's not what I was told when I bought the ticket," I said.

"Next," said the ticket agent, looking mildly irritated, nodding at the person behind me in line to approach the counter.

For about an hour I tried to find a loophole or workaround. I spoke with several members of airport security. I found a fireman who worked at the airport and pleaded my case. It was all to no avail.

"DAD, IT'S NO BIG DEAL," said Charlie. "I'll be fine. I can find the gate." Weeks later Charlie told us that he was freaking out during this ordeal. But at the time he seemed calm.

"We'll talk to you on your cell phone while you find your gate," I said.

"You told me to leave my cell phone at home," Charlie said, looking slightly irritated. It was true. Charlie's cell phone did not have international service, so I had prevailed upon him not to take it. It was part of my ongoing battle to free my boys from the clutches of technology so *I* could talk with them.

CHARLIE HAD TO GO NOW if he was going to make the plane. All the plans and money would be down the drain if we cut bait now. Charlie got in line to go through security. Susie and I followed alongside, talking to him, but on the other side of the security fence.

"Maybe there's a pay phone up by his gate," I said to nobody in particular. I wasn't sure "cell phone Charlie" even knew what a pay phone was.

I grabbed a handful of change from my pocket, called Charlie over, and handed it to him through the fence.

"Call me when you get to your gate," I said.

"Okay," he said. He returned to the line, and began putting his shoes and belt into the grey plastic bin for security scanning. He was a little distance away now. We watched from the fence as he cleared security, put his shoes and belt back on, then checked his boarding pass and passport.

"Charlie!" called Susie "Go to Gate 303 and call Dad from the pay phone." Tears flecked her cheeks.

Charlie was about fifty feet away now, on the other side of security. He heard Susie, turned, looked, found us. He smiled, gave us a thumb up, turned, and headed down the concourse. We stood and watched his yellow shirt disappear into the crowd.

TWENTY MINUTES LATER MY CELL PHONE RANG.

"Dad I'm at the gate," Charlie said. "We board in half an hour."

"Call me back when you're ready to board," I said. "Talk to Mom for a minute."

"Dad I can only talk for like one minute," he said. "That change you gave me was all pennies and nickels."

"Get some more change and call me in half an hour. Now talk to Mom." I handed the phone to Susie. They talked for a few seconds.

WE WAITED FOR CHARLIE TO CALL AGAIN. It was taking a long time. My cell rang.

"Charlie, are you ready to board?" I asked.

"This is a recorded message from Blockbuster. Your movies are…..

ANOTHER CALL WAS COMING IN! I tried to dump Blockbuster and catch Charlie's call but was too late—it went to voicemail. A minute later I retrieved it. We huddled around the phone and listened to Charlie's recorded voice.

"We're boarding now," Charlie said. "Goodbye … Oh …. almost forgot….. Love ya and that kinda stuff….. Okay bye."

His tone was flat and he sounded a little scared.

Dear God be with him. Charlie was on his way to Istanbul!

WE FOUGHT TRAFFIC BACK TO MANHATTAN and got to our Holiday Inn on 57th St. about 6:00. After dinner we walked to the Richard Rodgers Theatre on West 46th St. where we had tickets for the musical *In the Heights*. It's a great show, something of a modern day *West Side Story*, about the New York neighborhood of Washington Heights during the power blackout of 2003. Tom and Will loved the Latin music and hip hop dancing.

"It shows that a musical can be both contemporary and relevant," said Tom. Pretty insightful for a sixteen year old—I thought. Two years earlier, we had seen *Phantom of the Opera* a couple blocks from here. When Tom got home he started playing the music on the piano. We signed him up for piano lessons, and he got serious about music.

After the show we walked down to Times Square, then back to our hotel. Susie and I had a drink at the bar and talked about Charlie. He was well into his flight by now. We went back up to the room, watched a little *Late Night* with the boys, and crashed.

MY CELL PHONE WOKE ME AT 3:00 a.m.

"We've got Charlie and he's just fine," said Chris Melink.

I was half asleep, hugely relieved, and a bit overwhelmed. I choked out a thank you and then Charlie came on the phone. The flight had gone fine. He sounded tired. Chris came back on. He said they had some fun plans.

"Tomorrow they were going to mess around with some cars," he said.

I thanked him for getting Charlie and we said goodbye. *Mess around with cars.* What was that about?

SUSIE, WILL, TOM AND I had a great couple days in New York. Our family chemistry changes, often for the better, by removing one person. On Sunday we went to mass at St. Ignatius Loyola on 84th St. My great grandfather Wilhelm Schickel was the architect and it is truly magnificent. Will and Tom found the plaque that marked the pew where John and Jackie Kennedy used to sit. After Mass I photographed St. Ignatius for the new book on Dad's work—which included some family history for context.

We went for breakfast at a restaurant near St. Ignatius and got a good lesson in Turkish politics. Our waiter was Greek. Susie, who once had a Greek boyfriend, got the lay of the land long before I did. On learning that I was a fireman, the waiter was friendly, and asked what we were doing in New York. Susie saw immediately where the conversation was going, and tried, unsuccessfully to stop me. When I told him that our youngest son was going to Turkey, his friendliness stopped abruptly. He glared at me and muttered something that was phonetically garbled but metaphysically clear:

"How could you send your son to be with *those people*?"

I tried to regroup, and explained to the waiter that Charlie was not staying with Turks, but with Americans who happened to live in Turkey. Too late. He was storming off to calculate our bill, which was higher than I expected.

"Turks and Greeks don't like each other," said Susie when we were safely outside on the sidewalk. "Get it?"

WE WALKED IN CENTRAL PARK in the afternoon. Near Columbus Circle I checked out two possible venues for exhibits of Dad's work—the Museum of Biblical Art (MoBiA) and the Museum of Arts & Design (MAD).

It started to rain as we headed for the hotel, and

Susie ducked in a gift shop on 57th St. Will, Tom, and I wandered into the bike rental next door. It interested me because in my pre-fireman days I started and ran a bike rental business—the Loveland Bike Rental—on the Loveland Bike Trail. It was great little business, fun to operate, and it still exists today. In the 1980's Dad would put down art projects to help me take care of bike rental customers.

"You know what I like about the bike rental business?" Dad asked me once, while pumping up a bike tire.

"What?"

"Much less bullshit than the art business."

Amen to that!

The young owner/operator was Turkish, friendly, and had a great location just a block from Central Park. Business was good. He was excited to hear about Charlie's trip to Turkey. Thomas asked him about Turkey/Greece relations—and told him a bit of our experience with the Greek waiter earlier that day. The man told Tom there were many old hostilities—but emphasized that these were part of the past—not something he felt or was interested in.

Then he told us his own story of arriving a few years earlier at Kennedy Airport—penniless and alone — searching for opportunity. A few years later here he was part owner of a small business—doing pretty well. It was the classic story of the American immigrant. What a wonderful story for the boys to hear—first hand.

I GAVE DAD A CALL as we waited for Susie to finish at the gift shop.

"New York is an amazing classroom," I said to Dad when he picked up. I filled him in on things. He was especially interested in St. Ignatius and the museums I had visited.

"Where are you right now?" Dad asked.

"I'm standing outside a bike rental on 57th St. This guy's got a good location near Central Park."

"How are his prices?" Dad asked.

"A little higher than ours," I said. "But I'm sure his rent is higher."

"You never paid me any rent," said Dad.

I changed the subject.

WE TOOK A CAB TO DINNER that night. The driver was from the Dominican Republic and lived in Washington Heights, the neighborhood that the play *In the Heights* is based upon. I asked if he had seen the play. He laughed and said he had not, but he had heard about it.

"In my hometown in the Dominican Republic the electricity goes out every day and its no big deal," he said. "In Washington Heights the electricity goes out once in twenty years, and somebody writes a big Broadway Play about it. And you know what I say about that?" he asked.

"What?"

"That's America!" he said.

WE LEFT NEW YORK on Monday afternoon. Our van emerged from the Lincoln Tunnel in a driving rain. A couple hours into Pennsylvania Susie took a call from Erin Melink, Colin's mom, in Istanbul.

"They had a blast with the cars," she said to Susie.

Everything was going fine and she had exciting news. Charlie had arrived in Istanbul just ahead of newly elected President Barack Obama, who was touring several countries as part of the European Economic Summit. There had been a reception at an Istanbul hotel—and since Colin's dad worked at the American Embassy they were able to attend. They had just met, and shaken hands with, President Obama, halfway around the world. The cars that

FACE TO FACE

Chris had been talking about were the cars in the Presidential motorcade.

Joseph Schickel

18. Summer

Spring had busted out and summer was coming on strong! Its natural forces hit our house on the Little Miami River like the arrival of a new beauty queen at a small town high school. It wasn't *an* event; it was *the* event!

It was a beautiful Saturday afternoon. Dad and I sat on the front porch drinking Jim Beam, talking, reading, and enjoying the sounds of summer. Bees buzzed frantically in the wisteria, dogwood, pear, and honeysuckle blossoms in our yard and along the river. Lawn mowers groaned and the smell of cut grass was in the air. The river came alive with canoes, inner tubes and the cries of young, often medicated, human floaters.

THINGS WERE LOOKING UP. Dad was still weak, but he had made it through the winter. With warmer weather and more walking he would surely gain strength. He was excited about his new paintings. He talked about his next exhibit and flogged me to keep the book moving.

Susie resigned as music director at St. Veronica's —a good and long overdue move which allowed us to go to Sunday mass together, like a regular family. She had lots of private music students, and come fall would teach music, theatre, and co-direct the show *Annie* at Leaves of Learning.

Will was about to graduate high school. His graduation party was fun. We enjoyed hearing his classmates, friends, and teachers reminisce about the high school years.

Tom was thrilled to be releasing his debut album *Living On*, with seven original songs. We scheduled an album release party for June 9 at the Works. Two UPS boxes arrived at the house with the albums, cellophane wrapped, inside. Pretty cool! Dad was very excited about Tom's musical accomplishments, and was looking forward to the release party.

Charlie was in the afterglow of his Turkey trip and ready for sleeping in, swimming, playing basketball, going to Kings Island, hanging out with friends, and avoiding chores by staying out of earshot of his parents.

Susie and I were about to celebrate our twentieth anniversary on June 3. We had a family Outer Banks vacation scheduled for July. John would once again stay with Dad when we were gone. It was going to be a good summer!

COCK A DOODLE DOOOOO!" said Dad's incredible talking wristwatch.

"Dammit, I need you to reset this thing for me," said Dad.

I got him a splash of whiskey, then retreated to the basement, found the instructions for the wristwatch, and tinkered with it until it seemed to be back on track. I returned to the porch and handed it to him, and asked him to try it out. It seemed to be working. I could tell Dad was feeling bad about having to ask us to do so many things for him.

"I sing a song called *I Need*," said Dad.

"Is it a love song?" I asked, trying to humor him.

"No, it's more a pain in the ass song," he replied.

I laughed, or at least I tried to.

THE SMELLS OF SUSIE'S COOKING AND SOUNDS OF TOM'S PIANO drifted onto the front porch. Horse flies smacked the screen as Will came up the walk. He was muscular, bronze, shirtless, and made the river mud he wore look good, or at least better. His Aussie Swagman hat was jaunty and his shoes made a squishing sound.

"Take those muddy shoes off before you come inside," I called to Will. He sat on the porch steps and removed the rancid sneakers.

"Where have you been, Will," asked Dad.

"Working at the canoe livery," replied Will. "In the river mostly. It was really busy today."

"I'm looking forward to your graduation," Dad said. "I hope I can make it down there."

"Thank you Grandpa," said Will. "I hope you can too."

"That was a great graduation party," said Grandpa.

"Thanks Grandpa," said Will. He went inside to

shower.

TOM CAME ON THE PORCH AND SAT with Dad and me.

"Tom, I am so excited about your album release," said Dad.

"I am too, Grandpa," Tom said.

"It's quite an accomplishment," said Dad.

"I guess," said Tom.   The conversation languished.   He went back inside and played the piano.

"SHOULD WE READ A LITTLE *NORTH OF HOPE*?" I asked Dad.

"I'd like that," he replied.   "But first get me a little more whiskey."   I found the worn paperback, and replenished his glass.

Jon Hassler's book *North of Hope* is an old favorite from my college days at Saint John's University in Minnesota, where Hassler was writer in residence. It's about the arrival of lovely, lively Libby Girrard at Linden Falls High School in rural Minnesota.   There she meets thoughtful, pious Frank Healy who is thinking about becoming a priest.

"Remind me where we were," said Dad.

"Libby was asking Frank about his mother's

death," I said.

I STARTED READING. Frank speaks first:

"At first I was glad I got there too late to see her die, but now that I'm older I wish I'd been there. I mean her last words were about me, and I should have been there to hear them."

"What were they?"

He cleared his throat nervously, and Libby saw a tenseness come into his eyes. "She said, 'I want Frank to be a priest.'"

How horrible! Thought Libby. "Who told you, your dad?"

"No, Eunice told me."

"Did you believe her?"

At this, he turned to Libby, nonplussed. "Believe her? Why shouldn't I?"

Libby shrugged. "I just wondered. It's so—you know—such a serious thing. You'd want to be sure she got it right."

"I asked my Dad if those were her exact words. He said he came over to the bed too late, and all he caught was the last word. It was 'priest' all right."

They drew close to the school and slowed down to avoid a group of classmates who were dawdling along the sidewalk and seemed to be waiting for them to catch up.

Libby asked quietly, "Will you be?"

"Will I be what?"

"You know." The word "priest" was hard for her to bring out. It weighed too much.

"Will I be a priest?" He looked troubled. *"If it's my decision, it's hard to know what to do."* Then he brightened a little. *"But if it's my mother's, then it's easy."*

Her sense of horror deepened. She'd never heard of placing one's life in the hands of the dead. *"Frank, can I tell you something? You're not making sense."*

He didn't reply. He looked away.

"It's quite a story," said Dad. "Frank's got some deciding to do. Remind me who Eunice is."

"She's the rectory housekeeper who became a second mother to Frank after his real mother died," I said.

"Frank needs some space to think for himself," said Dad. A motorcycle roared by. "There goes some lady," said Dad, sipping whiskey, and feeling good.

Susie called us for dinner. I steadied Dad as he transferred from his chair to the scooter, then held the door for him as we made our way to the table.

19. Reds' Game

On Friday of the 29th Week in Ordinary Time, also known as June 5, in the year of Our Lord 2009, it was just Dad and me for the morning meeting at the Church of What's Hap'nin' Now, so we kept it informal.

The first scripture reading (Tobit 11: 5-15) told the story of blind old Tobit who is finally able see his son Tobias again (and presumably his wife Anna also, though this is not mentioned) after many years. Tobias cured his father's blindness by smearing his eyes with the gall of fish, and then pulling off the white film.

"Quite a story," Dad said after I read it to him before breakfast. "I sure wish I could see better."

"Maybe we should call Dr. Bell again," I said. Dr. Howard Bell was Dad's excellent ophthalmologist. We both knew Dr. Bell wasn't offering much hope at this point with Dad's macular degeneration.

Dad was in good spirits. It looked to be a beautiful day. He was still fighting a cold but was hugely grateful for *warm weather*.

"How are the Reds doing?" Dad asked as I perused the morning *Enquirer*.

"They're a game above 500." I said. "They beat the Cubs yesterday."

WE HAD BEEN TALKING ABOUT GOING TO TONIGHT'S REDS' GAME, and Dad probably sensed that I had mixed feelings about this. I was feeling overwhelmed by work and family stuff. Going to the Reds' game was an idea Dad wanted to stir into flame. He was afraid it would die on Joe's back burner.

"Who's pitching tonight?" Dad asked.

I found the preview for tonight's game.

"Micah Owings," I said. "Never heard of him."

"He'll probably be the next Dizzy Dean," Dad said. Yeah, yeah, yeah.... I could see where this was going.

IN DOWNTOWN CINCINNATI, construction workers on the fortieth floor of the Great American Tower, which was soon to be Cincinnati's tallest building, dawdled on the Ohio River side and looked down into the Great American Ballpark, where the grounds crew was setting up the batting practice. In Cincinnati people like to talk about *Great American* this and *Great American* that. After several Hudepohls beers everybody's a *Great American*. The rest of the world is three drinks behind, and we wish they would catch up!

IT WAS A BEAUTIFUL EVENING FOR BASEBALL but I didn't have a good feeling about going to the game. Besides the baseball game there was a Keith Urban concert downtown. I was worried about traffic, parking, handicapped access, taking Dad to the restroom, and him getting cold. But we headed out taking two cars, so Dad could leave early. Dad and I in were in my Taurus. Susie and the boys were in the van.

Dad was in a great mood, and we listened to Marty Brenneman's pre-game warm-up on WLW Radio on the way down.

"It's great to be out," he said. "I really appreciate you taking me."

Traffic downtown was terrible, and we came to a complete standstill about a mile from the stadium. From the Red's website I had printed off sheets showing handicapped parking. It became obvious that I would not be able to get anywhere near these. My fears were being vindicated.

"Dad, maybe you and I should go home and watch the game on television," I said.

Silence.

"What do you think, Dad?" I nudged him again.

"We're down here, let's go to at least part of the game," he said.

Silence. We are going to the damned game!

To get out of traffic I drove up Main Street away from the riverfront, then came back down on Race, jumped a low curb and found a questionable parking spot under an overpass near Third Street. I was glad we took two cars because Susie would not have approved. I told Dad to sit tight while I searched my trunk for cover. I hung a Cincinnati Firefighters uniform shirt in the window, and made sure my Local 48 stickers were conspicuous. Then I hung Dad's handicapped sticker from the mirror.

I got Dad's wheelchair from the trunk and brought it around to him. He had the car door open, and his legs swung out, waiting for me.

"I'm ready," he said. "Hold it steady."

Dad got aboard and we headed out. The next ten minutes were amazing. Dad smiled broadly, as we rolled down the gentle incline toward the stadium. Every curb had a ramp, every person got out of the way. We spotted Susie and the boys right away. A friendly usher, seeing the wheelchair, guided us to a newly opened ticket window where the service was immediate and gracious.

The friendly woman selling tickets glanced at the wheelchair and said, "I have just what you need." On the stadium map she showed me a special section right under the smokestacks in center field with excellent wheelchair access. She handed us the ticket and we were off. Friendly ushers rushed to clear a path and before we knew it we were sitting in great seats between the smokestacks in center field. Dad and I had just gone from our parking spot on Fourth Street to great, inexpensive seats without encountering a single significant wheelchair obstacle.

"THEY THOUGHT YOU WERE MOSES," I told Dad.

"What do you mean?

"You just parted the Red Sea!"

"What did you expect?"

The Cubs center fielder tossed a ball into the stands just to our right. Charlie raced toward it but was too late.

"Joe doesn't believe in miracles, Dad," said Susie.

"I know he doesn't," said Dad. "But I do."

"So do I," chimed Susie brightly, the little suck.

"I believe in lucky sons o' bitches," I muttered under my breath.

"Do we have to bring Dad along next time?" asked Tom. "He's really grumpy and we're trying to have a good time."

My Dad laughed and laughed like that was really hilarious.

"Let's just leave Joe at home next time," Dad said to Tom. "He doesn't like baseball anyway."

Luckily, I was now halfway into my first tall cup of beer, which told me to shut up and take my beating like a man. I believe in miracles, but that's between me and my Budweiser. Let the do-gooders bray about their piety! The beer was going about its appointed task, and the edge was coming off.

"Play ball!" I shouted after the National Anthem.

"Joe, could you give me an idea of where the field is?" Dad asked a few minutes later. He was seated between Susie and me, and the field was directly in front of him.

WE HAD A GREAT TIME. Dad couldn't see much. But he loved the crack of the bat, the roar of the crowd, the cool breeze off the Ohio River, and being out and about with family.

"Cold beer here!" called the vendor.

"Should we get a beer?" Dad asked me. He apparently didn't realize that I already had one. I switched it to the hand away from him.

"I don't think so," I said, wishing to avoid the restrooms (and the more embarrassing alternative) if possible.

"We should have brought a flask of Jim Beam," he said. I chuckled and Susie looked grim.

"Look at the new building going up," Susie said, wanting to change the subject. "It's going to be the tallest building in Cincinnati."

"Where is it?" Dad asked. He was always intrigued by a new building, and we had been reading about this one in the paper.

"It's just outside the stadium, Grandpa" said Tom. "It's kinda right in front of you."

"Is that the one Gyo Obata designed?" Dad asked. Gyo Obata was founding architect for the St. Louis architectural firm Hellmuth, Obata, Kassebaum. Dad knew Gyo Obata in his after-college days, and did art commissions in a number of Obata buildings.

"Yes," I replied. "He was quoted in the *Enquirer* recently in an article about this building."

"He said they're going to put a tiara on top," said Susie. "Look, you can already see the beginning of it." We looked at the new building, which was starting to dominate the skyline. A silver curved metal structure was coming together, in the sorta, kinda shape of a tiara.

"A tiara on a building," Tom said incredulously. "Let me think." I could hear his brain humming. "It's like putting a roof on a prom dress."

"Or a minaret on a synagogue," said Susie.

"Or a pagan obelisk in the middle of St. Peter Square," I said.

"Or a biblical image on a totem," said Dad.

Pause.

"That isn't cheesy," said Will, breaking the silence. "That's cool… kind of inspired."

Susie explained what she had read recently in the *Enquirer*. Architect Gyo Obata had announced at a press conference that the top structure of the building would be a tiara. He had gotten the inspiration from Princess Diana.

"Now that's cheeeeeeesy!" said fearless culture critic Tom Schickel.

"No wonder he struck out with your mother!" Dad said to me, sounding smug.

"*What!?*" said Susie, Tom, and I simultaneously. He had our attention now. Dad went on to explain that when he was courting Mom in St. Louis, famous architect-to-be Gyo Obata "came calling" at Mary's home.

"He never had a chance," said Dad, making a hand gesture toward the Cincinnati skyline that he could not see as if to say "What kind of woman would marry a man who would do that!"

THE REDS GAVE UP A RUN IN THE FIRST INNING and another in the fifth. Pitcher Micah Owings pitched six innings, gave up five hits and two earned runs, and took the loss, bringing his record to 3-7. Dad and I left when they pulled him, and headed for the car, which mercifully was not towed.

"Dizzy Dean, eh?" I said as I helped him into the

front seat.

"One game does not a career make," he replied solemnly, plopping into the seat.

We listened to the last two innings on WLW radio, and Dad enjoyed announcer Jeff "The Cowboy" Brantley's drawl. Dad could follow the game itself much better on the radio than anywhere else. In the eighth inning the Reds scored a run and threatened to take the lead. But the rally stalled and the inning ended with the go-ahead run on second base.

The Cubs beat the Reds 2-1. The game was just getting over as we arrived home. I pulled in the driveway and wheeled Dad up the ramp and inside. He had to go to the bathroom right away so I helped him onto the toilet, then went to get his glass of wine and night meds.

We sat together in his room and talked. He said how much he had enjoyed the game and thanked me for taking him.

"Should we read a little *North of Hope*?" I asked.

"Sure, if you're up for it," he said. I fetched the weathered paperback and found my bookmark.

"Remind me where we were," he said.

I reminded him that associate pastor, Father Frank, was visiting the pastor, Father Adrian, who had suffered a heart attack and was in the hospital.

We pick up the story as Fr. Frank walks into Fr. Adrian's hospital room:

Adrian, wired for core readings, was lying still and breathing evenly. His eyes were closed. There was a dribble of urine in the bag. Of the medical crew, only the pretty, cream-haired young woman remained, standing by the window in a shaft of light.

"He seems much better now," she said musically. "Let's hope the worst is over."

Frank nodded, allowing his eyes to linger on her for a few moments, arrested by her beauty. Her hair, aglow in the sun, was a halo.

A little later, Fr. Adrian wakes up and talks with Fr. Frank:

"Frank,"

"Adrian. How are you feeling?"

"Fine. A little sleepy."

Frank patted his hand. "You can sleep all you want."

"It's my heart, isn't it?"

"It is. Some damage, the doctor says, but you're doing much better."

There was a long pause—Adrian gathering strength to continue. "Frank I saw an angel."

"You did."

"Yes."

"I wasn't delirious, Frank."

"No."

They were getting me settled in bed and I looked over there and saw her. Just for a second."

"I did, too, Adrian."

The head rolled back, the eyes settled on Frank, then slowly went shut. "I'd like to know her name."

There were more conversations as the morning wore on, not about the angel. The numbers held steady. The doctor seemed encouraged. Bishop Baker phoned. A volunteer brought in the mail—a dozen get-well cards from Linden Falls.

Frank took his leave at noon. On his way past the nurses' station he asked the cream-haired girl what her name was. She said it was Cindy.

Dad laughed and laughed. "Quite a story," Dad said. "Is the author still alive?"

"No, Jon Hassler died about a year ago."

"Wasn't he up at Saint John's in Minnesota when you were there?"

"Yup."

We said night prayer together. He said again how much he enjoyed the game. I wished him a good nights sleep. He asked me to come check on him in a little while and I said I would.

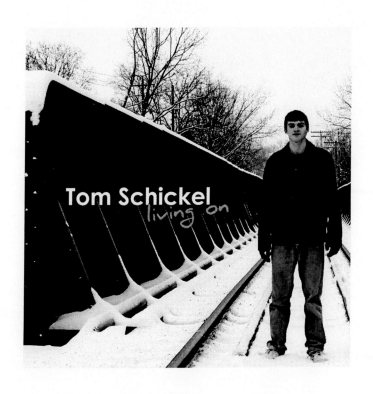

Tom Schickel
living on

20. Living On!

It was a warm Sunday afternoon in June, and the release party for Tom's debut album *Living On*, which contained seven original songs, was only two days off. I was in my bunker right underneath Dad's room working on photos for Notre Dame Press and monitoring Dad a little closer than usual. Dad had finished his nap, and I could hear him coughing and rattling around above me.

On Friday night we had gone to the Reds game and he seemed to be gaining strength. But on Saturday his cough and cold got worse and we feared pneumonia. Sunday morning he had a fever. We skipped mass and I took him to the Bethesda North emergency room, thinking there was a good chance he would be admitted. But his fever dropped by the time we got there and the chest x-ray was negative for pneumonia. Dad and I got home at 11:30, just ahead of Susie and the boys, who brought bagels and communion from the 9:45 mass.

Above me I heard Dad take a phone call from my sister Ruth in Michigan. They talked and laughed for a long time and I could tell Dad really enjoyed it. Tom started playing piano in the front room, practicing for the Release Party. I became engrossed in computer work again and was surprised to hear the unmistakable electronic sound of Dad's scooter being turned on, followed by the squeak of rubber wheels on the wood floor. Dad was pretty weak. I was surprised that he was leaving his room.

I went upstairs a few minutes later. Dad had pulled his scooter up near the piano and was listening to Tom play. He wore his usual black cap and his nearly sightless eyes were closed. His head was bowed and moving slightly to the music. I snapped a couple photos.

Tom, with unkempt hair spilling out from under his cap looked, in the unbiased opinion of *this* papa bear, like Bob Dylan on the cover of *Nashville Skyline*. His hands moved comfortably across the keys of our old upright as he sang a dirge he wrote called *Shadows of Time*.

And I'll hear their sweet voices again and again
And there's never a day that it ends
And I'll visit you always in the shadows of time
And I'll look to the stars and I'll call out your name
When you're gone...

The song ended with a progression of descending minor chords.

"That's just beautiful, Tom," Dad said after he finished. "Did you write that?"

"Thanks Grandpa," said Tom. "Yes, I wrote it."

"What's it about?"

"It's about my friend Ellie Sand, a classmate, who died in an accident," said Tom.

"It's quite a song," said Dad. He shook his head "I'm really looking forward to your album release party. I hope I can make it. I've been weak lately."

"I hope you can make it too," said Tom. "It's gonna be fun."

LET'S READ A LITTLE *NORTH OF HOPE*," I said to Dad. It was Tuesday, and we were back in the emergency room at Bethesda North Hospital. They did another chest x-ray and this time it was positive for pneumonia. Dad was getting admitted but there wasn't a bed available yet. We had been waiting for about three hours now, and Dad was getting agitated.

In *North of Hope* pretty Libby had found her first boyfriend at Linden Falls High School in the unlikely person of one DeVaughn Smith. DeVaughn played in the band, which gave him a *temporary* advantage over the football players. He could sit in the stands with Libby at Friday night football games.

I started reading.

"DeVaughn, I have to tell you something," said Libby, after the Willowby game, which Linden Falls lost 30-0. "You make being a boyfriend look like hard work."

"It is hard work, Libby." He was walking her home, briskly, for they were facing a cold night wind. "What makes it especially hard is that everybody tells me how lucky I am to be going with you."

"And you don't see it that way?"

"No offense, Libby, but I'm not crazy about dates. I'd rather stay home and practice my trumpet."

"Then that's what you should do, DeVaughn. You won't hurt my feelings."

"But I'm supposed to want to go on dates. That's what gets me down. Everybody else wants to go on dates."

"What do you care what everybody else wants? If you like music so much, then stay home and play music."

"I've been writing a sonata for trumpet for a year and a half. Maybe when it's finished, I'll like going on dates."

They kissed at Libby's front door on Pincherry Street. She patted him on the cheek and said, "Will you play your sonata for me sometime?"

"Sure. I might be done this winter."

"Let me know."

They kissed again, gingerly, and DeVaughn said good night and walked away. Then he stopped and called to Libby as she was stepping inside and shutting the door: **"It's got three movements with a coda at the end."**

DAD LAUGHED. "What a great story," he said, and then shivered.

"I'm freezing," he said. "Is there any way to turn the heat up?"

"I don't think so," I said. "I'll find you another

blanket."

"It shouldn't be like this," Dad said. "Call that nurse back again."

"Dad we just called her," I said. "There's not much she can do until a bed becomes available."

"It's very frustrating," said Dad. It was about 3:00 p.m. "I'm going to miss Tom's album release," said Dad. "I was really looking forward to it."

"Maybe he'll give you a personal concert when you get home," I said.

"He gives me a personal concert every day," said Dad. "Now where is that damn nurse? Can't they turn the heat up? I'm freezing!"

"I'll be back in a minute," I said. "I'll try to find her."

I WALKED OUT IN THE HALL, and called my brother John. He was on his way, but delayed by traffic. I told him I needed to leave by 4:00 so I could help Tom set up sound equipment for his performance that night.

"I should be there by 4:00," John said.

I found Dad's nurse, thanked her for her good work, and apologized for Dad being grumpy. I asked did she have any further word on when Dad's room might become available. Another hour. Could I take a warm blanket for Dad from the heater? Not a problem. I took a warm blanket, returned to Dad's bed, and tucked it around him.

"Thank you, that's much better," said Dad. His shivering stopped, at least for now.

"Dad, John will be here shortly," I said. "When he gets here I'm gonna leave to help Tom get set up for his gig at the Works.

"I understand completely," Dad said. "Tell Tom good luck, and how much I wish I could be there. It's a really big deal, his first album release. He's quite a kid."

John arrived, I left, and Dad got a room.

"IT'S TOUGH BEING A MUSICAN," Works owner Scott Gordon said to me. He lugged two buckets of ice to the bar as I wrestled an ancient speaker into place. Gangly Tom happily signed copies of his *debut* album for teenage girls.

"Tom has a good manager," I grumbled.

"Looks more like a *roadie* to me," laughed Scott. "And quit your belly achin'. It's a step above city council." Point taken. I was in my eighth year on Loveland City Council, and it was getting to be a grind.

I am grateful that Scott and Jamie Gordon, who

own the Works, accorded my son Tom (the hometown musician) and my Dad (aging artist and *pater familias*) personal project status for a few key years there. The attention and support Dad and Tom got when they walked *or were wheeled* through the door of Loveland's quintessential family restaurant and bar, is one of those amazing miracles of small town America. Watching Dad sip his vodka martini, offer Susie his olive, and move his black-capped head to the music while Tom performed at the Works is a memory I will always cherish.

The Works is located near the Loveland Bike Trail in an old red brick building that originally served as a water filling station for steam locomotives on the adjacent B&O railroad. In my more recent memory it was the public works garage for the City of Loveland. Salt trucks, mowers, and road equipment sat where the dining area, bar, and kitchen are now located. On city council, I was happy to support transforming our public works garage into a thriving, privately owned restaurant.

"Is your Dad coming?" asked Scott.

"He's in the hospital with pneumonia," I said.

"It's gotta be killing him to miss this," said Scott. "He loves to hear Tom play."

"He'll be back soon," I said. Oblivious in

retrospect.

THE PLACE WAS STARTING TO FILL UP. Beer taps flowed and plates clanked. Waitresses in black skirts smiled at customers and snapped at busboys as they rushed to deliver food and grab tips. At 6:30 Tom took his throne at the keyboard and asked his *manager* to get him a glass of water. There was a 45 minute wait for tables, not bad for a Tuesday night. He adjusted his harmonica holder, tapped the microphone with his finger, and kicked the evening off with the Billy Joel classic *Piano Man*.

There was a good burst of applause and a few hoots, led by the *manager*. Tom thanked the audience, then quietly vamped a simple chord progression and did his talking intro:

GOOD EVENING, my name's Tom Schickel and I'm a singer/songwriter from Loveland. I want to thank the **Works** *for having me here tonight. My debut album* **Living On** *can be bought for $10. I would be happy to sign it for you between sets. I will play the songs from the new album in my second set. Thank you for coming, stick around, and don't forget to tip your waiters, waitresses, and bartenders. They do a wonderful job, and the longer they're in business, the longer I'll be in business.*

And with that he launched into the rest of the

first set. It was a *cool* event. Tom's second set was all original songs and it went great. He performed a few songs with his friend Pete Stone, who co-wrote one of the songs with him, and these were especially well received.

"How's your Dad doing?" Pete's mom, Gretchen Stone, asked me, walking to our cars after the event.

"He got admitted to the hospital today with pneumonia," I said.

"Ohhhhhhh! I was wondering why he wasn't here." She paused for a moment, silent (unusual for Gretchen), stoical. "Pneumonia can be an old man's friend," she said.

Gretchen—now a medical doctor—and I were childhood friends. Susie and I and the boys are good friends with her, her husband, Phil, and their three children. About ten years earlier, the Stone family had moved from California back to Ohio, to care for Gretchen's aging mother, Nancy. We assisted the Stones in Nancy's care from time to time, but hadn't really understood the magnitude of their undertaking, until we took Dad in, which of course provided the proverbial two-by-four of wisdom up side the head. They did a magnificent job with Nancy, and offered valued advice and moral support in Dad's care.

ON THE WAY HOME I called my brother John to check on Dad. I had been planning to go back to the hospital after Tom's event, but was having second thoughts. I was tired.

"He's checked into his room and sleeping peacefully," said John. "There's no need for you to come tonight." It was all the encouragement I needed.

"I'll stop by in the morning," I told John, and he headed for Kentucky.

SUSIE AND I SAT ON THE FRONT PORCH. Tom sat with us long enough to count his tips, which were *good*, then retreated to the living room to join the post concert discussion on Facebook. Charlie shot baskets under the light in the back yard and Will played guitar upstairs.

It was a warm summer night. A motorcycle roared by and nobody said, "There goes some lady." Fireflies flashed in the dark, and a fisherman's kerosene lantern glowed down by the river.

"The boys are really looking forward to our vacation at the Outer Banks," Susie said.

"Me too," I said.

"Can I get you another hard lemonade?" Susie asked.

She could, and did, and got one for herself, and

they were really good and cold.

Dark shapes and low voices passed on the sidewalk in front of the house. We sat on the porch swing together and the hard lemonade tasted great. We had a little buzz going by the time the boys drifted back.

Tom did an imitation of Grandpa calling "Susie," then Charlie eclipsed it with an imitation of *his Dad* calling "Susie." We laughed pretty hard. Susie smiled and held my hand, and it was good to be sitting on the porch together.

"I can't wait till vacation," said Will. "I love the Outer Banks."

"Uncle John will stay here and take care of Grandpa again, right?" asked Tom.

"Right," I said.

We were concerned about Dad in the hospital, but at this moment, relieved to have a night together free of his care.

Joseph Schickel

21. Ora et Labora

It was a sunny, warm February afternoon in Rome, seven months after Dad died. Rifled and khakied carabinieri in army trucks bristled around the Aventine. Police manned barricades on the Via di Santa Sabina. Vatican security, with dark suits and high tech ear pieces, looked alert and efficient. Heads bobbed above ancient Roman walls as tourists and residents craned their necks to catch a glimpse of His Holiness Pope Benedict XVI, who was expected shortly. A modern day Zachaeus found a good spot in a sycamore tree, until Vatican security dislodged him.

It was Ash Wednesday, the Christian feast

marking the beginning of the season of Lent, forty days of fasting and prayer leading to the Last Supper (Holy Thursday), Crucifixion (Good Friday), and Resurrection (Easter Sunday). The Pope was on his way to bless the ashes and celebrate Mass at the Domincans' Basilica of Santa Sabina, the traditional "stational church" for Ash Wednesday.

The service actually begins at the Benedictines' Church of Sant'Anselmo, just a few hundred yards away. It is a fairly small church, seating about 350. The *Litany of the Saints* is sung as the Pope and his entourage make their way in procession down the walled Roman street to the Basilica of Santa Sabina, which is much larger. My old friend Fr. William Skudlarek, OSB, monk of Saint John's Abbey in Minnesota, now working in Rome, had managed to get us in for the Sant' Anselmo service.

The church was almost empty when we took our seats, but quickly began to fill up with Benedictines and Vatican dignitaries, some of whom Father Tony —our good friend, guide, and travel companion on this trip — identified for us by name.

"Lots of skirts but not many women," groused Susie.

It was revealing to see cardinals, whose scheming caricatures are so provocatively promoted on television (*The Tudors*) and in popular fiction (*The Da Vinci Code*) just a few feet away, standing between pews, and clumsily pulling robes on over their heads. They joshed, cajoled, and straightened each other up. The mystique was gone. They were old men putting on uniforms for a parade. It could have been the American Legion on the Fourth of July! One dropped his glasses. Another needed help with a safety pin. Susie, hard-wired Catholic girl, tried to jump in and help but I held her back. There had been a crazy lady attack on the Pope and a cardinal at Christmas. We were probably in the crosshairs of a carabiniero's riflescope up in the balcony.

By 4:00 p.m. the church was nearly full. There were over thirty Cardinals, many bishops, a good number of priests, a couple of nuns, and lots of Benedictine monks, who *ora*ed and *labora*ed at Sant' Anselmo. There were about twenty lay (non-ordained) people (including five Schickels) and ten women (including Susie).

A gaggle of young Cistercian monks in black and white robes landed breathlessly in the pew behind us, giddy to see the Pope. The place was full now. A helicopter was heard overhead, and Vatican security went into super duper lockdown mode. Pope Benedict was about to enter.

"You American?" asked the young Vietnamese monk standing behind my son Tom.

"Yes, American," said Tom, smiling, being gracious, and shaking the monk's eagerly extended hand. Later he would comment that the Vietnamese boundaries for personal space are closer than our own.

"Ahhhhh, my friend also American," said the monk, and he introduced Tom to the monk next to him.

"Where are you from?" the American monk asked Tom, shaking his hand.

"Loveland, Ohio," said Tom.

"Do you know the Robinsons?" he asked.

"Of course; they are my cousins," said Tom.

In the seconds before Pope Benedict's entrance, Tom and the young Cistercian figured out that they were second cousins, who knew and recognized each other from family events. Father Tony, Susie, and I watched this little drama unfold with drop-jawed disbelief.

"The Vietnamese monks will think that America is a very small place," Father Tony said later, laughing and shaking his head.

The Vatican version of *Hail to the Chief* began on the organ, the back doors opened, everyone turned around, and Pope Benedict entered with his entourage. They processed down the center aisle, passing a couple feet to our left. Sleek digital cameras emerge from monastic robes in the pew behind me, and I was emboldened to shoot a couple pictures myself.

The Pope went first to the Eucharistic Altar on the right, where he knelt and prayed for a few moments, then took his place at the presiding chair at the back of the sanctuary. There were a few short readings, followed by the *Kyrie*, sung in Greek, to the same melody we used at St. Columban when I was a kid.

Kyrie eleison, sang Pope Benedict.
Kyrie eleison, responded the congregation.
Christe eleison, he sang.
Christe eleison, we responded.

Next came the *Litany of the Saints*. It is a beautiful prayer in which the cantor sings out the names of long list of saints, one by one. The congregation responds to each name with a simple request to that saint—*pray for us*—sung in Latin, the words are *ora pro nobis*. I remember it well from my pre-Vatican days as an altar boy.

Santa Maria, Mater Dei, sang the cantor.
Ora pro nobis, we responded.
Santa Maria, Mater Ecclesiae,
Ora pro nobis.
Omnes sancti angeli et achangeli,
Orate pro nobis.
Omnes sancti patriarchae et prophetae,
Orate pro nobis.
Sancte pater Abraham,
Ora pro nobis.
Sancte Joannes Baptista,
Ora pro nobis.

The *Litany of the Saints* continued and the Papal procession to the Basilica of Santa Sabina began. A processional cross and candles led Cardinals and then the Pope down the center aisle past us, and out the back door of the church. Next came Benedictine monks and Vatican dignitaries seated in the front of the church. And then, to our surprise, security directed us to join the Papal procession.

"Just keep walking and singing," said Father Tony under his breath. "Act like you're supposed to be here."

Ora pro nobis, we sang with more conviction as we

joined the procession.

The Pope's white hat bobbed thirty yards ahead of us we processed down the narrow drive of Sant' Anselmo. The procession widened when we got out on the street, and we walked only ten yards behind the Pope.

"Why are they waving at us?" asked Charlie, referring to the people on the *other side* of police barricades, waving Papal flags, and watching the procession.

"Because they think we must be important people," said Tom "Now shut up and sing!"

Susie was in shell shock, Father Tony smiled in rye disbelief, Will swaggered like he was finally getting the respect he deserved, Tom was serious, and Charlie was like *this is no big deal when are we gonna eat?*

> *Sancte Benedicte,*
> *Ora pro nobis.*
> *Sancte Antoni,*
> *Ora pro nobis.*

DAD DIED ON JULY 14, 2009, five weeks after Tom's album debut on June 9, which was the same day Dad was admitted to Bethesda North Hospital for pneumonia. Seven months later we took a family trip to Rome, partially at Dad's behest. It was something we had talked about and wanted to do for a long time.

When Dad was near the end I found myself thinking about that amazing nun, Sister Norberta, on the deck of the German ship *Deutschland* as it foundered in a winter storm off the coast of England in December of 1875. "Christ, come quickly," she had prayed aloud when the end was near. Dad's storm was different, but no less difficult, and we prayed the same prayer.

For some reason when I think about that nun, I picture her as Sister Mary Dorita, SND, who was principal at St. Columban Grade School back in the 1960's. She was as intrepid a nun as ever silenced a classroom roiling with smart-ass, foul-mouthed, snot-nosed, pimple-faced, hormone-crazed, clueless Clermont County Catholic eighth graders. We thought we were hot shit, but we were just a nasty bunch. It was a misconception she corrected many times before. She brooked no quarter, and would have stood tall in a shipwreck. She and her SND cohorts were *outstanding selfless educators*, and I am hugely in their debt.

North of Hope was the last book Dad and I read

together. We never finished it, but we read it a lot in the last two months of his life, including once on the morning of the day he died, and it always buoyed his spirits.

When people asked Dad why he was Catholic he sometimes responded, "Because it's the air that I breathe." As I hope this book has testified—Susie and I and the boys have been the beneficiaries of some very good Catholic air. God breathed on the water, and I guess he breathed on us too.

We sang Dad into glory, then buried him next to Mom in the Grailville cemetery, in the caskets Tom and I had stumbled across in the barn several years earlier. I was his executor, as I had been for Mom. Philip Ping, who married our neighbor Bridget Hill and bought our old farm, made their caskets from the wood of the big old oak in Mom and Dad's back yard.

Phil's woodworking operation stands in that part of our old barn that was once the Shop, where Dad and his compadres and comadres created art, drank strong coffee, and had amazing conversations about everything under the sun. No bias here, but that art was pretty good too, and can still be seen throughout the Midwest and a few other places. A touring museum exhibit *William Schickel: Spirit Made Manifest* may be coming to your area soon.

Dad milked the cow in the back of the barn (the Shop was in the front) every morning and night. He carried the bucket into the house where Mom strained the milk, put it in gallon jars, and put it in the Frigidaire. The cream rose to the top and we made butter. It sounds romantic, but I hated churning butter. I liked hauling manure much better. It makes me think of the old milkman Tevy in *Fiddler On The Roof.* To use his words, we were poor as church mice, and so happy we didn't know how miserable we were.

Dad liked to have thing organized, and he liked to know what the plan was. A few hours before he died Susie sat at his bedside, held his arm, and talked with him, as he lapsed in and out of consciousness. They were great friends and had a wonderful rapport. Dad was very quiet for a long time. And suddenly the spirit of the Pegboard was in the room, and he looked directly at Susie and said very clearly, "What's the plan?" And Susie had the presence of mind to respond, "You're going to glory Dad."

And of course he did. And I'm sure he's enjoying getting reacquainted with Mom, Vince Hill, Dan and Mary Kane, his brother Norbert and lots of other saints.

"PLAYSE SPEAK AEINGLISH when ya order yer drrrrinks," barked the kilt clad bartender in exasperated brogue, as he drew two frothy steins of amber ale from the tap. Blonde German sisters, who had just struggled with their drink orders, blanched at his bark. He slammed the steins on the bar in front of them, and shot them a toothy grin.

"First one's on the house," he said. "Yer always welcome at the Fiddler's Elbow."

The girls laughed, tipped him a couple euros, and carried off their drinks

Will had found this very cool and hard to find pub—where English speaking expats, American students studying in Rome, and other miscreants hang out. It was open mike night. There was enthusiastic applause for a Scottish girl who had just finished a beautiful rendition of *Wayfaring Stranger*.

"Our next act is Tom from the USA," said the announcer.

Tom played *Piano Man,* which people loved, then he and I did *Knockin' of Heaven's Door* together.

> *Mama take this badge off of me*
> *I can't use it any more*
> *It's gettin' dark, too dark to see*

FACE TO FACE

Feels like I'm knockin' on heaven's door
Knock knock knockin on heaven's door
Knock knock knockin' on heaven

The table in front of us had cast from *Riverdance*. They hooted, clapped, and sang along. *Knockin on Heaven's Door* is one of the first songs Tom and I ever played together—and it was a cool moment.

IT WAS A WARM EVENING in Trastevere. The narrow, crooked alleys and ancient, walled streets were alive with people walking. Torches flickered and waiters holding menus stood outside *trattorias*. Scooters shumped cautiously over cobblestones, mixing with foot traffic, and occasional automobiles. Young couples held hands and talked quietly as they walked.

After dinner we got gelato and then Father Tony headed back to the hotel. He had an early flight back the next day, and we were staying for a couple more days. Susie and I sat in the *Piazza di Piscinula* near the Tiber and talked while the boys bartered with street vendors.

"It's still Susie and five guys," I said. "If you count Tony."

"He's been a wonderful guide," she said.

Tony was a huge help on our Rome trip. He had been to Italy many times, and is a natural teacher and guide. We ambushed him by proposing our Rome trip at a time that partially overlapped one he had already planned. The ploy worked and he agreed to be our guide for several days. His long friendship first to Susie then to our family has been a blessing over many years, and was especially important during the years Dad lived with us. Dad's care stretched our family at times, and Tony's friendly encouragement and steady support were *invaluable*.

"I hope we're not driving him crazy," said Susie.

Will returned from the street vendors with a scarf that had the colors of Loyola University Chicago, which he planned to attend the next fall, with an ROTC scholarship.

"Tony is an incredible teacher," said Will. "We do drive him crazy but he also enjoys it."

"He likes us," said Tom, who had just returned with Charlie from unsuccessful bargaining with street vendors. "Go figure?"

"He's a wonderful friend," said Susie. "We are so lucky, so blessed."

Amen. What she said!

IT WAS TIME TO GO. The boys were drifting back toward the street vendors, so Susie called them together, and we headed out. A saxophone played in the distance as we crossed the bridge at Tiber Island. Then we walked to the Argentina neighborhood and caught the bus to Termini.

Joseph Schickel

SHARING A BOOK

Dad's painting *Sharing a Book* is pictured on the opposite page.   Susie, Dad, and I read these books together in the two years Dad lived with us.

The Power and the Glory, Graham Greene

Exiles, Ron Hansen

The Measure of a Man, Sidney Poitier

Cold Sassy Tree, Olive Ann Burns

Clericalism: the Death of Priesthood, George Wilson, SJ

A Painted House, John Grisham

North of Hope, Jon Hassler

We were also regular readers of the *Cincinnati Enquirer, Image, America,* and *Commonweal.*

Joseph Schickel

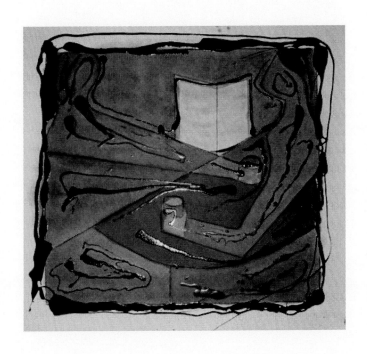

MUSEUM EXHIBIT

WILLIAM SCHICKEL
SPIRIT MADE MANIFEST

The traveling museum exhibit *William Schickel: Spirit Made Manifest* was produced by Katharine T. Carter & Associates, the University of Notre Dame Press, and the William Schickel Gallery.   Karen S. Chambers, Scott W. Perkins, and Joseph Schickel are curators. The second edition of book *Sacred Passion: the Art of William Schickel* by Gregory Wolfe with commentary on many of the exhibited works, is available at the museum gift shops, from the *University of Notre Dame Press (call 1-800-621-2736)*, at local bookstores, and at the *William Schickel Gallery*. No photography permitted. Contents Copyright *William Schickel Gallery* 2010. All rights reserved. Museums interested in this exhibit should contact Joseph Schickel at the *William Schickel Gallery*.

William Schickel Gallery
200 W. Loveland Ave.
Loveland, Ohio 45140
513.296.3967
www.WilliamSchickelGallery.com

WILLIAM SCHICKEL
SPIRIT MADE MANIFEST

williamschickelgallery.com

ktcassoc.com

undpress.nd.edu

pricetower.org

noelartmuseum.org

biblicalarts.org

Price Tower Arts Center, Bartlesville, Oklahoma
Oct. 1, 2010 - Jan. 9, 2011
Ellen Noël Art Museum, Odessa, Texas
Jan. 22 - Mar. 27, 2011
Museum of Biblical Art, Dallas, Texas
May 1 - Oct. 31, 2011

BOOK: Sacred Passion: the Art of William Schickel

The second edition of
Sacred Passion: the Art of William Schickel
by Gregory Wolfe was a finalist in
Foreword Review's
2010 Book of the Year Award.

Available at the
William Schickel Gallery
Online Giftshop.

www.WilliamSchickelGallery.com

Joseph Schickel

THE ART OF WILLIAM SCHICKEL

SECOND EDITION

Gregory Wolfe

Foreword by James Martin, SJ

sacred passion

BOOK: What a Woman! Mary Frei Schickel

This book is William Schickel's tribute to Mary Frei Schickel, his wife and lover for over sixty years. He wrote it shortly after her death in 2007. The late Father Matthew Kelty, OSCO, monk of Gethsemani wrote, "If you must read just one love story read this one."

Available at the
William Schickel Gallery
Online Giftshop.

www.WilliamSchickelGallery.com

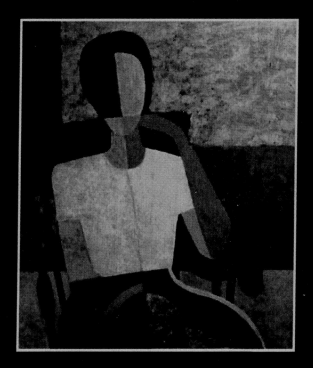

Mary Frei Schickel

What a Woman!

*A husband's tribute to his wife
and lover of sixty years.*

William J. Schickel

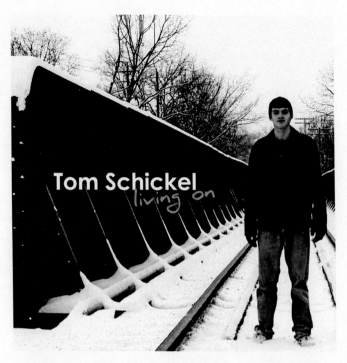

MUSIC CD: Tom Schickel: Living On

FOR MORE INFORMATION OR TO
PURCHASE THIS ALBUM ONLINE
VISIT
www.TomSchickelMusic.com
also available at the
William Schickel Gallery Online Gift Shop
www.WilliamSchickelGallery.com

William Schickel Gallery

The *William Schickel Gallery* in Loveland, Ohio exhibits and sells works by the late artist William Schickel and other artists.   Director Joseph Schickel is literary and artistic executor for William Schickel, and curator of the traveling museum exhibit *William Schickel, Spirit Made Manifest.*   Hours are by appointment, call 513.297.3967

WILLIAM SCHICKEL GALLERY
200 W. Loveland Ave.
Loveland, Ohio 45140
www.WilliamSchickelGallery.com
513.297.3967

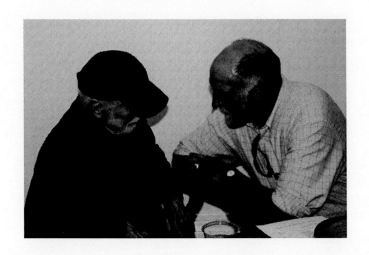

THE BOOK

FACE TO FACE

Conversations with my Father

IS ALSO AVAILABLE ON

KINDLE